D1642400

THE CRIME ARCHIVES

INSIDE THE MINDS OF TODAY'S DEADLIEST CRIMINALS

DAMON WILSON

SEVENOAKS

CONTENTS

INTRODUCTION

It is a common belief that crime is running rampant in modern society. It isn't. In fact, on almost every measurable scale, the rates of most types of crime have been falling remarkably quickly over the past several decades.

There are multiple reasons for this change for the better. For instance, some crimes fall out of fashion. The roads and parks of eighteenth century Britain were plagued by highwaymen like Dick Turpin. These wandering armed robbers were so common that Members of Parliament used to have to form into protective groups before risking the walk home through London's Green Park after nightfall. Yet the highwayman is nowadays as much a piece of dead history as the Cornish shipwrecker and the Roman gladiator – thanks mainly to the invention of the professional police force.

The highwayman didn't just disappear, of course. He transformed into the modern street mugger and house burglar. But even for muggers and burglars, times are changing. Burglary was rampant in most western cities in the 1980's and 90's, for example. Yet in the last decade it has dropped-off dramatically. The reason being, simply, that the resale value of portable items like TVs, DVD players and microwave ovens has gone through the floor. Why risk a prison sentence or an irate home-owner for items worth only a few pounds?

The police report that criminals are now turning to mugging rather than burglary: mugging takes just a few moments and a mobile phone, and a wallet or handbag, bring the criminal a good rate of return. But even that can't last. The increased use of CCTV on the streets, and the sophisticated security features built into the next generation of mobile phones, mean that the street mugger will soon find the risk is not worth the meagre profit that they get from the crime.

But what of the more serious crimes covered in this book? Murder; serial murder; spree killing; kidnapping/enslavement; and terrorism? As an author on criminology for more than 20 years, I can say with confidence that all of these sorts of criminals have been under siege, with a resulting fall in the crime rates.

In the case of murderers (like Phil Spector and Jane Andrews) and kidnappers (like Josef Fritzl and O J Simpson) increasingly sophisticated police forensic techniques and the commonality of security systems – like CCTV and computer record cross-checking – make getting away scot free increasingly difficult.

Of course spree killers and suicide bombers (like Thomas Hamilton and Richard Reid) have no fear of prison because they intend to die. But such people are increasingly being picked-up, before they commit their terrorist acts, by a combination of enhanced security techniques and the fact that members of the public are more attuned to spot – and report – the abnormal behaviour that leads up to these crimes.

But what of that bogeyman of modern society: the serial killer? I personally think that in ten or 20 years time, the serial killer will have gone the way of the highwayman. Advancements in psychological profiling mean that a good scene-of-crime officer can often spot tell-tale signs that can indicate, say, the age, habits, social background and previous criminal experience of a killer before any other clue has been gathered. Add to this the high likelihood that a serial killer will leave DNA evidence on a victim, and a successful identification and arrest becomes very likely. To be tagged as a "serial killer" a murderer must kill at least three people over a protracted period of time. In the future it is very unlikely that a killer will escape after one murder, let alone three.

The problem, as I see it, is not so much crime (which is falling, and will continue to fall) but our overpowering fear of it. Over the 1990's, for example, violent crime fell in the USA by 20 per cent. Yet media coverage of such crime rose by a factor of 600 in the same period. And that, remember, was before the advent of 24-hour news channels. Little wonder so many people feel surrounded by criminals, when almost every serious crime from around the world is reported and repeated by every news outlet.

A modern citizen needs to be informed enough about crime to know how to best avoid becoming a victim, and how to help the police fight criminals. People do not need to be constantly fearful. Some of the removable items in this book, such as the letters written by Robert Pickton or the note penned by John Allen Muhammad and John Lee Malvo, provide a horrifying insight into the criminal mind, but others reveal the hardwork and determination of the police and legal systems from around the world who bring these people to justice.

I hope you find the following cases informative, but don't let them worry you.

DAMON WILSON

LEFT The handcuff storage board at Stateville Prison, Illinois. It is a happy fact that police clear-up rates against serious crime continue to rise across the globe. Nowadays, crime just doesn't pay like it used to.

PHIL SPECTOR

Phil Spector was in his teens when rock and roll music swept first the United States and then the world. His father had committed suicide when he was ten, and three years later his mother moved the family from the Bronx area of New York to Los Angeles. By the time he was 19, Spector was already in a rock band, The Teddy Bears. Acting as the band's singer/songwriter and producer, he landed them a recording contract in 1958. His song "To Know Him is to Love Him" was inspired by the epitaph on his father's tombstone, and the single immediately went to number one in the charts and sold over a million copies.

The Teddy Bears' popularity declined quickly, however, and Spector gave up performing and songwriting to become a full-time music producer. He invented an orchestral, multichannel tone that was entirely new to rock music; he called it "The Wall of Sound". Through this he became one of the most influential music producers of the 60s and 70s – working with The Ronettes, The Righteous Brothers, Ike and Tina Turner, The Rolling Stones, The Beatles and The Ramones. But, for all his skill, he was also well known in the record industry for his quirky temper.

Spector's career dwindled in the late 1970s and was not helped by his increasingly eccentric reputation. It was even alleged that he once threatened The Ramones when they tried to leave his house. Johnny Ramone is reported to have said of the incident: "... he reaches into his jacket pocket and well, he pulls out a gun, puts it on the table right in front of us, and says, 'You guys don't really have to go yet, do you?'"

On 3 February 2003, Spector had himself driven to the House of Blues music and restaurant venue in West Hollywood. There he met Lana Clarkson, a B-movie actress whose career had taken a dip in recent years. Her most famous role – the lead in *Barbarian Queen* – had been back in 1985. Now, at the age of 40, Lana's acting opportunities had dried up; so, a month before she met Spector, she had taken a job as hostess in the House of Blues to help make ends meet.

Spector, who was apparently quite drunk, badgered her to come home with him, but Lana was evidently reluctant. She let herself be persuaded, however, and climbed into his chauffeur-driven limousine. A few hours later, in the early hours of the morning, Spector staggered out of his house and told the chauffeur: "I think I killed somebody."

The police were called and found Lana

ABOVE Phil Spector and The Ronettes in the early 1960s. Spector always understood the power of image. For most of his career he sported dark glasses whenever he was out in public; in the end they became a virtual brand image for the successful music producer.

ABOVE AND ABOVE RIGHT The crime scene photos of the body of Lana Clarkson: a revolver had been placed in her mouth and fired, killing her instantly. A fading actress and nightclub hostess, she had apparently been hesitant to accept Spector's invitation to go home with him.

RIGHT Police arrive at Spector's home in the elite Alhambra district of Los Angeles. Fully living up to the image of an eccentric music industry legend, Spector lived in a 33-room, mock-Pyrenees castle.

hallway. She had been killed by a single shot from a snub-nosed Colt Cobra revolver, fired at point-blank range into her mouth. The holster for the gun was found in a drawer nearby. Arresting officers had to use an electric stun gun to subdue Spector.

Spector told investigators that Clarkson had "kissed the gun" and committed 'accidental suicide". This remained his defence when he was tried for her murder in March 2007. However the judge declared this a mis-trial when the jury remained hung at ten members to two – the two jurors refusing to be convinced of his guilt.

At a second trial in 2008, the jury found Spector guilty of second-degree (unpremeditated) murder. The deciding factor seemed to have been the testimony of five separate women, all of whom told the court that Spector had threatened them at gunpoint when he lost his temper. Another witness, a bodyguard, testified that he had heard Spector ranting that all women were "f****** c***s" who deserved to be "shot in the head". The 68-year-old Spector was sentenced to 18 years to life in prison

BELOW Spector's rap-sheet photograph. Aged 65 at the time of his arrest, Spector still maintained his flamboyant image. He covered his baldness in court with a series of outrageous wigs, apparently unworried that this might annoy the judge.

SPLIT OPINIONS

It was not only the jury at Spector's first trial who was split in its judgement over his guilt. His own family apparently cannot agree on whether he killed Lana Clarkson. His wife, Rachelle stood by him, saying: "I've lost my husband and my best friend. I feel that a grave injustice has been done and from this day forward I'm going to dedicate myself to proving my husband's innocence." On the other hand, Spector's son Louis is reported to have said: "I'm torn about this. I'm losing my father who is going to spend his life in jail. At the same time, justice is served."

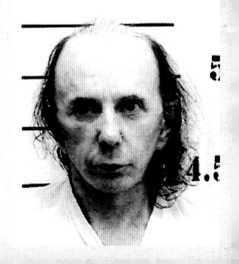

ARMIN MEIWES

Armin Meiwes was a lonely, 40-year-old German computer technician. He wanted to meet someone special, so he did what many people do if they come from a community or social group that can't fulfil their relationship needs – he turned to the internet to find a partner. Specifically, Armin wanted somebody to eat.

He found a website called "The Cannibal Café" that catered to those who shared his interest. Meiwes ignored the site's disclaimer – about maintaining a safe separation between fantasy cannibalism and the messy reality – and placed a "lonely hearts" advertisement, stating that he was "looking for a well-built 21- to 30-year-old to be slaughtered and then consumed". To his gratification he received many interested replies, but almost all of these turned out to be frivolous people who weren't really prepared to "go all the way". And Armin was a reasonable man who certainly didn't want to make a potential partner do anything against their will.

The only correspondent who was seriously willing to meet with Meiwes was Bernd Jürgen Brandes, a 41-year-old homosexual with a fetish for mutilation. On 9 March 2001, he arrived at Meiwes' suburban house in the small village of Rotenberg, near Essen in western Germany, and the pair hit it off immediately.

With a video camera running to capture the events in his specially designated "Slaughter Room", Meiwes tried to bite off Brandes' penis. It was actually Brandes who insisted that Meiwes use his teeth, so he was presumably disappointed when his partner found the living tissue too gristly to sever. He did, however, manage to crush both Brandes' testicles with his teeth. Meiwes then used a knife to finish cutting off Brandes' penis. Both men attempted to eat it raw, but this also proved too difficult – Brandes complaining that it was too "chewy". So, Meiwes sautéed the penis in Brandes' own body fat with a little salt, pepper and garlic. Unfortunately, the penis still proved too gristly to consume and they gave it to Meiwes' dog to eat.

All this time, Brandes had been partially anaesthetized with painkillers and alcohol, and had been lying in a bath in the "Slaughter Room" to avoid bleeding everywhere. Meiwes, who evidently did not relish killing someone by hand, gave him an overdose of sleeping pills and a bottle of schnapps and retired to wait for his partner to pass on. He read a *Star Trek* novel for three hours, then decided that enough was enough and killed Brandes by stabbing him in the throat. He hung the corpse from a meat hook, gutted and cleaned it, and removed chunks of meat for later consumption. Meiwes even attempted to grind down the bones to make ersatz flour for baking.

In December 2002 a college student alerted the German police after seeing a new advert for an edible partner posted by Meiwes; this gave the true details of his previous relationship with Brandes. Meiwes was arrested and police found what was left of his former partner in a deep freeze, hidden beneath pizza boxes. They also found a two-

ABOVE Meiwes' house in the village of Rotenberg, near Essen. The large building had more than enough spare space for Armin to design and build a "Slaughter Room".

hour video of the edited highlights of their "affair". It was estimated that Meiwes had already eaten 20 kilograms (44 pounds) of Brandes' flesh by the time of his arrest.

Prosecutors faced a problem in charging Armin Meiwes: cannibalism is not a specific crime under German law... and can one even be accused of murder if the "victim" was begging to be killed? The case rested on whether Brandes had been in a fit mental state to request his own death, and whether Meiwes had killed him purely because he had been asked to, or had done it for his own sexual gratification.

On 30 January 2004, Meiwes was convicted of manslaughter and sentenced to eight years in prison. However, prosecutors felt that this was a ridiculously lenient sentence and, moreover, sent out entirely the wrong message to other would-be cannibals. They successfully pressed for a retrial on a charge of murder. On 10 May 2006, Armin Meiwes was convicted of murder and sentenced to life imprisonment.

REDEMPTION?

Amwin Meiwes has made efforts to redeem himself while in prison. He is reported to have helped police analyze two other suspected cannibal murders and, commenting on his internet fans, said: "They should go for treatment, so it doesn't escalate as it did with me." He has also become a vegetarian.

TOP Meiwes (second from the right) during his compulsory military service. He had a domineering mother who insisted on accompanying him on dates with girls, and even turned up to oversee him when he was out on military exercises.

ABOVE Meiwes' "Slaughter Room", where Bernd Brandes died. The room was designed with tidiness in mind – with tiled walls and the bath to minimize the mess when Meiwes butchered his guest.

LEFT Armin Meiwes (pronounced "My-vuhs") in jail. Unlike other cannibal killers, Meiwes never intended to kill and eat unwilling victims. It was only through meeting with Brandes, who wanted to be tortured and eaten, that he became a murderer.

CHRISTOPHER ADAMS

At 11:25 am on 26 April 2005, North Cornwall Emergency Services received a call from a payphone. The male caller told the switchboard: "There's been a murder. She's been beaten around the head. The baby's had a plastic bag put over its head." He then gave the crime scene as Trewinnick Cottage in the tiny village of St Ervan. When the police operator asked what exactly had happened, the man simply said: "I don't know. I haven't got a clue. I found her in the back bedroom. She's lying on the bed. There's blood everywhere. She's my girlfriend and fiancée." Then he rang off.

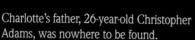

ABOVE Chris Adams was a likeable, good-natured man: loving to his girlfriend and a doting father, he worked hard to support his little family... until he killed them for no reason that he could later explain.

LEFT DCI Andy Boulting and Superintendant Chris Boarland report on the hunt for Christopher Adams. Another officer said o the case: "We've all got families and this is probably the most devastating sort of crime for anybody to come across."

The first emergency vehicle to arrive was an ambulance, driven by paramedic Mike Ford. It was only as he pulled up outside that he realized with horror that it was the home of the parents of his daughter's fiancé. Ford's partner prevented him from entering the cottage as arriving police officers hurried in.

In the bedroom they found the walls and ceiling spattered with blood. Mike Ford's 9-year-old daughter, Claire, was lying in bed having suffered severe blows to the head. Nearby was Claire's 18-month-old daughter, Charlotte, with similar cranial injuries. A bloody cricket bat was lying on the floor. A plastic bag had been placed over the baby's head and taped closed around her neck. Both victims had been dead for some hours.

Charlotte's father, 26-year-old Christopher Adams, was nowhere to be found.

A nationwide hunt was launched to find Adams. After making the telephone call to the emergency services (some five-and-a-half hours after the time of the murders) he had driven off in his mother's car. Over the next week he was seen twice – near Exeter in Devon and later near Bristol. Both times he was spotted at motorway service stations, which suggested that he was sleeping in the car and keeping on the move. He was eventually caught in Hampshire and made no effort to resist arrest. As police handcuffed him, Adams said: "I don't know what happened, mate. I just lost it."

Adams freely admitted to both of the murders. He said that the night before the

killings he had hardly slept because the baby had kept waking up and crying. At around 6:15 am he got up to give Charlotte her bottle then woke Claire.

He went on: "I suppose we had a falling-out. We've had falling-outs before. Nothing major. Nothing violent. Usually about the hours I work and things like that.

"Claire got up. I pushed her down. The bat was there. I just swung round to hit her with it. I don't know why I did it. I hit her again. I brought it back round and hit Charlie. I didn't mean to do it."

Everyone who knew him, including Claire's family, said that Christopher had always been a dedicated and loving partner and father, never showing any inclinations towards violence. So why had he lost his temper so

ABOVE Adams on the run, caught by a security camera at the Exeter service station, eight hours after the murder of his family. He doesn't seem to have had any plan for escape, but simply ran until he was caught.

BELOW Claire Ford and her daughter Charlotte "Charlie" Ford. Christopher was seen by those who knew him as the image of a loving and supportive father. And even he could give no clear explanation for the double-murder.

violently? The autopsy showed evidence of not just two impacts to Claire Ford, as he had described, but a positive rain of blows directed at her head and upper body. And if he had accidentally hit baby Charlie with the bat, then why had he then deliberately suffocated the infant?

During the subsequent trial, Christopher Adams refused to enter a plea of diminished responsibility owing to temporary insanity – despite the fact that, given his previous clean record, such an explanation might well have reduced his charge to manslaughter. He doggedly insisted that he was guilty of murder, although he still could give no substantial reason for the killing of his family. He received a life sentence.

A BROKEN-HEARTED KILLER

Sentencing Adams to life imprisonment, with a minimum tariff of 20 years, Judge Graham Cottle said: "The devastation that you have brought upon the lives of those who loved and cherished Claire and Charlotte is quite incalculable." Cottle added that he might have insisted that Adams serve a minimum of 30 years, but he had taken into account Adams' self-evident shame and horror. His guilty plea to murder – rather than attempting to wriggle out of his responsibility for the deaths or to try for a manslaughter verdict – saved Christopher Adams a possible extra ten years in prison.

SCOTT PETERSON

In late 2002, the Petersons were living a comfortable life in the town of Modesto, California. Scott, aged 30, and Laci, 27, had been married for five years and managed very well on Scott's income as a fertilizer salesman and Laci's wage as a substitute teacher. Best of all, their first child was due to be born in early February 2003. Then, on Christmas Eve, Laci disappeared.

Scott told the police that he had gone fishing for the day, taking his boat out from the marina at Berkley; when he returned home that evening his wife was missing, leaving behind her car, her mobile phone and her purse. Laci's only known plan for that day had been to go to buy some groceries and to walk the dog in the nearby park. The police immediately suspected that Mrs Peterson had met with foul play – eight-month pregnant women do not wander far from home without money or transport.

The press soon got hold of the story but Scott refused to give interviews, insisting he was too upset. However, the police almost immediately decided that he was the prime suspect in Laci's disappearance. Away from the public eye, investigators found Scott too relaxed and even prone to laughter – hardly the image of an anxious husband. He had also taken out a $250,000 life insurance policy on his wife, so stood to gain substantially if the police were forced to proclaim her "missing, presumed dead".

A neighbour told police that she had seen Scott leave the house on the morning Mrs Peterson vanished; Laci had not been with him but, ominously, Scott had loaded something heavy into the trunk of his truck before driving away.

Then a woman came forward to reveal that Scott Peterson was not the model husband that friends and relatives had previously believed him to be. Amber Frey, a 28-year-old single mother and massage therapist, had met Scott the previous November. They had started a love affair but Scott had failed to tell Amber it was adulterous. As soon as Amber saw Scott on television, described as Laci Peterson's anxious husband, she put two and two together and rang the police.

As forensic teams continued to check Scott's truck for signs of transporting a corpse, Scott reacted by casually selling his missing wife's car to buy a replacement for his impounded vehicle. He was also reported to be making enquiries with local estate agents about selling the house. He appeared to think his wife wasn't coming home.

Laci's due date, 10 February 2003, came and went with still no sign of her. It took a further two months before there was a development in the case, but when it came, on 13 April, it was macabre. The decayed corpse of an eight-month-old male foetus washed ashore just south of Berkley Marina, where Scott had gone fishing the day his wife vanished. The next day the headless, limbless

ABOVE Scott Peterson's Ford F150 pickup truck and his Gamefisher fishing boat, shortly after being impounded by the Modesto Police Department for forensic examination. Unfortunately, perhaps because this was over a week after Laci's disappearance, no evidence was found.

body of Laci Peterson was found near to where the baby had been found.

The police arrested Scott Peterson shortly after the bodies were discovered. Despite having heard the gruesome news, he was calmly playing golf when officers came for him. He had grown a beard and dyed both it and his naturally brown hair blonde. He was also found to be carrying $10,000 – the legal maximum that can be taken over the border into Mexico without having to notify officials.

The circumstantial case against Scott Peterson seemed damning, but the police had failed to find any physical or witness evidence that he had been involved in the killings. The prosecution insisted that Scott had wanted to start a new life with Amber Frey and that Laci and the unborn baby had stood in his way so he had killed them, But this was only a theory; they had no direct proof.

Nevertheless, the jury found Peterson guilty of first-degree murder for killing Laci and second-degree murder for killing the baby. The judge took their recommendation and sentenced Scott to death by lethal injection.

ABOVE RIGHT Laci and Scott, pictured shortly before the murder. Friends and family regarded the Petersons as an ideal couple. If, as Scott later claimed, Laci had known all about his extramarital affair, she told nobody and showed no sign of unhappiness.

RIGHT Amber Frey had an affair with Scott, unaware that he was married and was about to become a father. Scott's promise to be with her more often after the New Year, suggests that he had already planned the murder of Laci and the unborn baby.

BELOW Berkley Police Department divers searching for the remains of Laci Peterson. It seems likely that Scott would have escaped conviction if he had used a better anchor to weight Laci's torso: it was only its discovery that proved that murder had been committed.

PHANTOM SATANISTS

If the prosecution's case against Scott Peterson was purely circumstantial, what his defence offered to the jury was little less than fantastic. Scott's lawyer told the court that roving, murderous Satanists might have kidnapped Laci as she walked her dog in the park: who else would so brutally murder a heavily pregnant woman? The jury did not agree with this theory, however, perhaps because of the total lack of supporting evidence.

JANE ANDREWS

Born in the Lincolnshire town of Cleethorpes in the UK, Jane Andrews had a deprived upbringing. Her father, a carpenter, was often out of work, so the family mainly relied on her mother's meagre income as a primary school teacher. For most of her childhood, Jane lived in a house with neither a bathroom nor an indoor toilet.

ABOVE Andrews (left) and the Duchess of York leave a New York restaurant in 1995. The British establishment regarded both women as "not quite the thing": Jane because she had been born working-class and Duchess Sarah because she behaved like a carefree celebrity.

In 1988, 21-year-old Jane was working as a clothes assistant in her local Marks & Spencer's store and was in no doubt that she would be a poor nobody all of her life. Then she noticed an anonymous advert for a "dresser" in a genteel lifestyle magazine, *The Lady*. Jane applied for the job.

She heard nothing more for six months, but then a letter arrived out of the blue: Her Royal Highness, the Duchess of York requested an interview with Miss Jane Andrews. At any other time and, arguably, with any other member of the Royal Family, Jane wouldn't have even squeezed her nose through the door, but Lady Sarah (nicknamed "Fergie", after her maiden name Ferguson, by the world's media) was remarkably fun-loving and easy-going. She and Jane hit it off immediately, and the schoolteacher's daughter from Cleethorpes was given the job of Dresser to the Duchess.

Jane soon became more than a servant and fashion adviser; as the years went by she became one of Lady Sarah's closest confidantes. She also hobnobbed with royalty, statesmen, diplomats, celebrities and multi-millionaires, so it wasn't too surprising that Jane dropped her Lincolnshire accent and became increasingly "posh". In 1989 she married a wealthy IBM executive, 21 years her senior, but the marriage broke up amicably after several years. Another break-up with a rich boyfriend a couple of years later was less pleasant. The man rang the police to report that Jane had "trashed" his flat in her fury.

Meanwhile the Duchess was up to her neck in debt, mainly because she seemed totally incapable of living within even a royal budget. In 1997 she was forced to sack most of her personal staff, Jane included.

Andrews was shattered by the rejection. Suffering from depression, she had difficulty finding another position, but eventually got a job selling silverware in a prestigious Knightsbridge jewellers – she must, however, have felt that she was falling away from the glamorous world that she had happily inhabited for nine years.

In 1999 Jane met Thomas Cressman, a rich, well-connected playboy, five years her senior. Andrews later claimed that Cressman was a sexual predator who tried to force her into anal sex, bondage games and bizarre role-playing – all of which she found abhorrent. She said that when she rebuffed him he threatened her and was capable of violence.

If this version of their relationship was true, then others – even close friends – saw no signs of Cressman's cruel behaviour towards Jane. On the contrary, it seemed to be Jane who was highly possessive of Tom, jealously fending off any women who looked even mildly interested in him.

In the summer of 2000 the couple went on holiday to the South of France. A friend later reported: "Jane asked Tom a blunt question about marriage, and Tom gave her a blunt answer. He didn't want a family with Jane because he thought that she was unstable."

Back in London, on the evening of 7 September 2000, Jane and Tom had a showdown. She later claimed that he attacked her, raped her and then accidentally fell on the knife that she was holding to defend herself.

The prosecution claimed that, infuriated by another refusal to marry her, Jane cracked Tom over the head with a cricket bat, went to the kitchen to get a carving knife, then stabbed the unconscious man in the chest, killing him. The forensic evidence supported the prosecution's case and the jury found her guilty of murder. Jane Andrews was given a sentence of 15 years to life.

FINGERPRINT
DO NOT TOUCH

ABOVE RIGHT The upper hallway in Jane Andrews's flat on the day after the murder of Thomas Cressman. Andrews later claimed that Cressman battered down a door to get at her, then raped her.

RIGHT The kitchen knife that killed Thomas Cressman. Andrews claimed to have stabbed him accidentally while defending herself but, again, forensic examination showed that she murdered the unconscious man in cold blood.

BELOW Andrews and Cressman in happier times. It is probable that Andrews saw their relationship as the only way that she could hang on to the privileged life to which she had become addicted. Others said she behaved with possessive jealously towards Cressman.

A BRIEF ESCAPE

Jane Andrews escaped from East Sutton Park open prison in Kent on Sunday 22 November 2009. After sleeping rough for a night, she phoned her aged parents in Grimsby and they hurriedly booked a taxi to make the 338-km (210-mile) trip to Kent. The taxi driver picked Jane up, muddy and dishevelled, from a deserted graveyard near the prison. Realizing who she was, he dropped his passengers off at a nearby hotel and immediately rang the police. Andrews was rearrested and placed in a secure prison.

TETSUYA SHIROO

Most Westerners imagine modern Japan to be a place of order and polite behaviour – a society that is well regulated to an almost bizarre degree – and in many ways this is indeed true. Yet it is also a fact that Japan is home to one of the world's largest organized crime syndicates, the Yakuza. According to the Japanese National Police Agency there are an estimated 84,000 members, which is a considerably higher figure than the American Mafia ever managed to field, even in their 1930s' heyday.

Identifying themselves with large and elaborate body tattoos, Yakuza members indulge in all the criminal activities traditionally associated with branches of the Mafia around the world: extortion, pimping, armed robbery, blackmail, people trafficking, drug dealing and the occasional murder or gangland turf war.

On the other hand, the Yakuza have at least a modicum of social responsibility in their psyche. Following the earthquake that devastated the city of Kobe in 1995, it was the local Yakuza gangsters who were first to get organized and start implementing disaster relief procedures. While the Japanese authorities dithered and delayed in the vital first few hours, the Yakuza were hauling people out of the rubble, distributing food and clean water, and even using a helicopter to reach cut-off areas.

On the evening of 17 April 2007, the Mayor of Nagasaki, Iccho Itoh, was outside his campaign headquarters, near Nagasaki train station. He was standing for re-election to a fourth term, having originally come to power in 1995, and remained very popular with the voters. Despite the election entourage, a stranger managed to walk up behind Itoh and fire two shots at point-blank range into his back. The mayor died of his injuries the following morning.

The killer was apprehended by Itoh's supporters before he could escape or hurt anyone else, and was then handed over to the police. He turned out to be Tetsuya Shiroo, a Yakuza boss of the Suishin-kai mob, this being a Nagasaki affiliate of the Yamaguci-gumi – the largest and most feared gang in Japan. (With an estimated 45,000 members, the Yamaguci-gumi is almost a

fifth of the size of the entire Japanese military establishment.)

Yet it quickly became clear that Shiroo was not acting on orders from his Yakuza superiors, and that the killing had no direct link to gangster activities. The television station TV Asahi handed over to the police a letter sent just before the assassination and written by Shiroo, which laid out his petty grudges against Mayor Itoh and his administration. It appeared that Shiroo's main gripe was that, while he was visiting a municipal construction site in 2003, his car ran into a pothole and was badly damaged. The gang boss was furious that the city government had refused to pay for the repairs. He also felt aggrieved because a construction firm, linked to the Suishin-kai, had lost out to another company when bidding for a city contract.

ABOVE LEFT Tetsuya Shiroo, the boss of the Suishin-kia mob. As a Yakuza kingpin, he could wield the power of life and death. But even he would, literally, bow to his Yamaguchi-gumi bosses in Tokyo.

ABOVE RIGHT Japanese scene-of-crime officers investigating the site of Mayor Itoh's murder. There was little to find since Shiroo used the traditional Mafia assassination method of getting in close and firing point-blank into his victim.

ABOVE The mourning daughters of assassinated Mayor Iccho Itoh entering the court carrying a photo of their dead father. Many people were shocked at just how powerful the Yakuza had secretly become in Japanese society.

BELOW A Yakuza mobster exhibits the traditional, all-over body tattoos that advertise a member's lifelong dedication to the crime syndicate. Yakuza regard such tattoos as a badge of honour – others see them as a warning sign.

Neither reason seems to justify a homicide, but Shiroo had clearly been mulling over his resentment until he had lost all sense of proportion. He told investigators that he had been planning the murder for almost three months, and they could find no evidence that any of his Yakuza henchmen had been in any way involved in the murder.

His trial began the following January, with his confession as the main evidence. Tetsuya Shiroo was condemned to death by hanging. This sentence was reduced to life imprisonment by the Fukuoka High Court in September 2009.

As a sign of their shame at their boss's action, the Suishin-kai announced its disbandment in 2007. Its members are believed to have been welcomed into other local Yakuza gangs.

BAD HAND

The members of the Yakuza are well aware that they are little respected outside crime circles, and their very name indicates this with a touch of bleak irony. The word *yakzu* is actually derived from the Japanese phrase "*ya, ku, za*," translating as "eight, nine, three". This, in turn, represents a losing hand in *Oicho-Kabu*: the Japanese version of Blackjack. In effect, the Yakuza are openly calling themselves "losers."

KENNETH NOYE

There can be few living British criminals who have remained in the public eye as long as Kenneth Noye. He first came to the media's attention following the Brinks Mat robbery at a Heathrow warehouse in 1983. Thieves, hoping to steal £3 million in cash, instead found and got away with £26 million in gold bullion and diamonds. Since they were simply thuggish armed robbers, they had no idea how to launder three tonnes of gold bullion, so they turned to Kenneth Noye – he had all the right connections.

On the surface Noye was a successful businessman: he owned a road haulage firm, was a Freemason and moved in well-to-do circles. But he also had several convictions for receiving stolen goods.

Noye had the gold melted down and recast, thus destroying the tell-tale imprints on the original ingots. It could then be sold above board with the authorities being none the wiser. The plan failed when the robbers used a single Bristol bank to move the resulting revenue. The bank informed the Treasury of the unusual activity and they, in turn, told the police.

Tracing the financial transactions to Kenneth Noye, the police put his country house under close surveillance, with two officers hiding in the garden. This proved to be a tragic mistake: one night in January 1985, Noye confronted them and stabbed PC John Fordham 11 times, killing him.

Noye was charged with murder, but his defence successfully argued that he had struck out in terror when Fordham, dressed in camouflage clothing and a ski mask, lunged at him out of the dark. Noye was found not guilty.

He was less lucky over his involvement in the Brinks Mat robbery. Found guilty of handling stolen goods (the bullion), he

ABOVE LEFT Kenneth Noye at the time of his arrest for the murder of Stephen Cameron. Many were surprised that an experienced criminal like Noye would lose everything over the "road rage" stabbing of a total stranger. That is, if Cameron was a stranger to Noye...

ABOVE RIGHT Daniella Cable and Stephen Cameron. Daniella showed considerable courage in first identifying Noye as Stephen's murderer in a police lineup, then giving eyewitness evidence against him in court. It was widely rumoured that nobody crossed Kenneth Noye and got away with it.

DOCUMENTS

ITEM 1

A card that Phil Spector sent to a friend, in which he insults the prosecuting District Attorney (and the D A's mother). The postcard reached the media and was an embarrassment for Spector's defence team; not least because it showed their client as rather immature and irresponsible.

ITEM 2

Extracts from the police search warrant issued for the search of Phil Spector's home. Such a warrant has to lay out the police reasons for suspicion that a crime has been committed. Even minor faults in such a document can undermine, or even halt, later court proceedings.

ITEM 3

Despite Jane Andrews's jealous behaviour, it seems likely that Tommy Cressman genuinely loved her. It was her continued insistence on marriage that seems to have driven him to consider leaving her: a decision that probably cost him his life.

ITEM 4

This receipt for petrol purchased by Peter Falconio was use by the prosecution at Murdoch's trial to prove that they was driving on the Stuart Highway before Falconio disappeared.

MISSING MILLIONS

Most of the Brinks Mat robbery loot was never recovered. In simple terms the £26 million haul of 1983 would probably be worth about four times as much in today's money, but the thieves would have lost a lot of its potential value in the laundering process. They are rumoured to have invested much of the resulting money in drug-smuggling operations, in buying an oil well in Kansas, and in swathes of property on the Costa del Sol and in London's Docklands. Most of these "investments" would have increased in value over the decades, making untold millions. And what about the gold itself? Three tonnes of bullion can go a long way on the open market. It has been suggested that any gold jewellery made after 1983 might well have a little of the Brinks Mat haul mixed into it.

served eight years of a 14-year sentence before being released in 1994. Most of the Brinks Mat loot had escaped detection by the authorities so there seems to have been a nice little nest egg waiting for Noye when he left jail.

Just over a year after his release, on 14 April 1996, Noye became involved in an altercation beside the M25 – the London orbital motorway. According to the prosecution when the case came to trial, Noye was at the wheel of his Land Rover when a van, driven by 17-year-old Daniella Cable, cut sharply in front of him. He followed the van onto a slip road and both vehicles pulled over onto the verge. Daniella's boyfriend, 22-year-old Stephen Cameron, confronted Noye, who, in a fit of "-road rage", drove a knife into the younger man's liver and heart. Stephen died in Daniella's arms while Noye drove off.

Kenneth Noye ran away to the Costa del Sol in Spain, but was identified and arrested in 1998. Extradited back to Britain, he stood trial in 2000, where he was found guilty and sentenced to 16 years to life in prison.

According to William Donaldson in the book *Brewer's Rogues, Villains and Eccentrics* (2002), there is another aspect to the killing of Cameron that neither the prosecution nor the defence mentioned at the trial. Donaldson claims that Cameron was a low-level drug dealer who knew Kenneth Noye; in fact he owed Noye money and the "road rage" row was actually about that – it had nothing to do with Daniella's driving.

Why would this potentially key piece of information be kept from the jury? The

defence would not have wanted a potential motive for murder to be aired, thus reducing their chance of an acquittal. And the prosecution would have wanted to paint Cameron as a totally innocent party, rather than somebody who appeared to be involved in a seedy drugs meeting by the side of a motorway that ended in a knife fight.

TOP Police officers search the grounds of Kenneth Noye's mock-Tudor mansion in Kent, following the killing of PC John Fordham. Noye escaped conviction for the killing, but could not escape the evidence that he had laundered the Brinks Mat gold and had it sold on the open market.

ABOVE A policeman guards the prison lorry that transported Kenneth Noye to stand trial for the murder of Stephen Cameron. Noye's extensive contacts with criminal gangs in and around London made the authorities fear an armed attempt to break him free.

COLIN THATCHER

On 17 December 1982 , Colin Thatcher, the Canadian Minister for Energy and Mines, resigned from the cabinet of the Conservative government. Usually the aftermath of such a setback for a politician is a period in the political wilderness, but in this case, within a week of his resignation, Colin Thatcher would be arrested as a murder suspect.

Thatcher came from a political family. His father, Ross, had clawed his way up the greasy pole from small town politics to become the premier of Saskatchewan, but Colin got little encouragement in his own political career from this dismissive and unaffectionate man.

Colin's success in government seems to have brought out the arrogant bully in him. Certainly his relationship with his wife, JoAnn, had been a happy one before he became a member for the electoral district of Thunder Creek in 1975, but thereafter he treated her with a mounting coldness that verged on contempt. Colin started staying out later and later, and JoAnn guessed correctly that he was seeing other women behind her back. She finally divorced Thatcher in 1980.

On the evening of 17 May 1981, JoAnn was standing in the kitchen of the house she shared with her new husband, Tony Wilson, when she was suddenly knocked to the floor. Someone out in the darkened street had shot her in the shoulder. She survived and the bullet proved to have come from a .303 hunting rifle, of the sort Colin Thatcher had recently bought. Although her ex-husband was an obvious suspect, the police made no effort to arrest or charge him. It was widely rumoured that he was being given political protection.

Thatcher's appointment as Minister of Energy and Mines in May 1982 further enhanced his conceit and pomposity. But

ABOVE Police remove the mutilated body of JoAnn Wilson from her garage. Neighbours had seen a man of Colin Thatcher's build lurking around the neighbourhood for some hours before the murder. He could not be positively identified however, because he had been wearing an evidently false beard.

TOP JoAnn Wilson, Colin Thatcher's ex-wife, photographed in 1980. Her right arm is held in an odd pose because she is wearing a steel brace under her clothes, after being shot in the shoulder by an unknown assailant.

over the following months his questionable political decisions, his arrogant self-importance, his unconcealed sex affairs and the persistent rumour that it was he who had shot JoAnn badly undermined his standing and embarrassed the Conservative government. Few people were surprised when Thatcher was forced to resign in January 1983.

Four days later, on 21 January, JoAnn Wilson was attacked as she got out of her car in her garage. Her assailant grabbed her by the hair and struck her repeatedly over the head with a heavy, bladed weapon, cutting ruts in her skull and, as she tried to protect herself, breaking the bones in her forearm and partly severing her left little finger. JoAnn fell to the floor and her attacker shot her in the head with a pistol.

Police naturally suspected Colin Thatcher, but had little to go on. Then an ex-criminal called Gary Anderson approached the police and freely admitted that he had known Thatcher had planned to kill his wife. In fact, Thatcher had tried to hire Anderson to commit the murder for him, but Anderson had refused.

Anderson, at the request of investigators, now contacted Colin Thatcher, claiming to be worried that the police might accuse him of the murder. During their phone-tapped conversation Thatcher came close, but did not quite admit, that he was the murderer.

Put on trial, Thatcher was initially charming and elder-statesman-like. But when prosecution lawyer Serge Kujawa suggested to him that defence witnesses, including Thatcher's sons, might have been persuaded to give false evidence, Colin flew into a raging fury. Bunching his fists he roared at Kujawa: "It's easy to say that my sons have lied. Why don't you step out of courthouse and say that where you don't have immunity?"

The jury were visibly shocked by this werewolf transformation: all the political smarm in the world could not whitewash over the impression that he was a man who could not control himself when annoyed.

Colin Thatcher was found guilty and was sentenced to life with a minimum of 25 years to serve. Nevertheless, he was paroled in December 2006 after serving fewer than 22 years in a minimum security prison.

ABOVE RIGHT Colin Thatcher under police guard in 2000. Despite the violence of the murder for which he was convicted, Thatcher spent much of his sentence in Ferndale Minimum Security Prison – one of the world's few prisons to boast its own golf course.

RIGHT Thatcher following his release in 2006. He continues to furiously insist on his innocence. He has written an autobiography called *Final Appeal: Anatomy of a Frame*, in which he claims that media bias and legal trickery was used to obtain his conviction.

A RIGHT MAN?

Maybe it was the unhappy relationship with his cold and dismissive father that made Colin Thatcher into what he author A E van Vogt called a "right man". Right men can be utterly charming, provided nobody dares to cross them; but if anyone that they consider an inferior contradicts them, they can fly into an irrational rage. They are "right men", because they cannot stand to be proved wrong.

BRADLEY MURDOCH

On 14 July 2001, Peter Falconio, aged 27, and his girlfriend Joanne Lees, 26, drove out of the town of Alice Springs in Australia's Northern Territory in their Volkswagen Kombi camper van. The couple, who came from Huddersfield, England, were in Australia for a holiday. The next day Lees was found calling for help on the Stuart Highway, her hands bound in front of her with makeshift handcuffs made from cable binders. Peter Falconio was nowhere to be seen.

Police soon found the camper van abandoned by the side of the road at a place called Barrow Creek, with no sign of Falconio and only a small bloodstain on the ground to indicate foul play. Joanne Lees claimed that a stranger had signalled them to pull over, indicating that something was wrong with their exhaust. Peter Falconio had got out of the van and walked around the back with the man while Joanne stayed inside. She heard a bang, like a backfire. Then the man had returned, armed with a handgun, and had tied her hands behind her back before throwing her into his pickup truck.

Luckily, Joanne said, she had managed to get away and hide in the scrub of the outback. The man had hunted her with his dog for five hours before giving up and driving off (presumably taking Peter Falconio's dead body with him). Aboriginal trackers examined the area immediately afterwards, but could only find Lees' footprints.

Initial media suspicion tended towards Joanne herself. In 1997 a woman called Tracie Andrews had been jailed for life for stabbing her boyfriend Lee Harvey to death by the side of a road in Worcester in the UK. Andrews had claimed that Harvey had been

killed by a stranger in a "road rage" incident, but forensic evidence had clearly indicated her guilt. Three years later that story seemed to be echoed in the version of events as told by Joanne Lees.

But then, in 2003, the Australian police made an arrest. Bradley Murdoch was a drifter and drug smuggler who had been in the Alice Springs area and apparently left at about the same time as Falconio and Lees, even taking the same road as them. Joanne identified Murdoch as her abductor, but it later transpired that she had already seen a photo of Murdoch on a website that had identified him as the police

ABOVE Police scene-of-crime officers search the area around Peter Falconio's abandoned VW Kombi van. The Stuart Highway, near Barrow Creek, runs through the northern outback – a vast area of scrub where a well-hidden body might never be found.

suspect, so her identification is somewhat questionable.

Rather more damningly, DNA tests found tiny amounts of Bradley's blood on the gearstick of the van, on the cable-tie handcuffs and on Lees' T-shirt. However, mix-ups in the forensic laboratory contaminated the samples of the first two, so it was only the T-shirt sample that was used in evidence.

The prosecution case was that Murdoch was a paranoid drug smuggler who had thought that Falconio and Lees were following him – acting on this suspicion, he had killed Falconio and was planning to kill Lees. The main evidence against him was Lees' (rather shaky) identification, and the one DNA sample that had not been accidentally contaminated.

The defence claimed that Falconio was actually still alive, and had faked his own death – hence the failure to find his body and the lack of evidence of a death by shooting. Murdoch, they said, was a fall-guy, arrested and framed by the police to cover their embarrassment at being unable to solve the case. This argument did not explain the DNA on Lees' T-shirt, however, and Murdoch was found guilty and sentenced to 28 years to life in prison.

Murdoch has since appealed the sentence on the grounds that the LCN (Low Copy Number) DNA test used to identify his blood on the T-shirt has been said to be unreliable by some experts. His appeal was rejected.

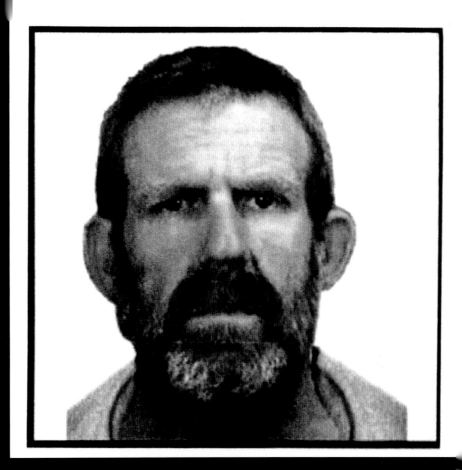

BELOW Joanne Lees and Peter Falconio about set off on their fateful road trip. The couple may not have been as happy as they at first appeared. During Murdoch's trial it was revealed that Lees had had sex with another man, Nick Reilly, while they were visiting Sydney.

ABOVE Bradley Murdoch – no relation of the media tycoon of the same surname – was a self-confessed drug-dealer and drifter. He has also showed a dangerous disregard for human life: in 1995 he served 15 months in prison for shooting at some people who were noisily celebrating a football match.

DEAD OR ALIVE?

Bradley Murdoch continues to protest his innocence, and there are certain anomalies to the case that are certainly worth questioning. Why did Joanne Lees not suffer from exposure after claiming to have lain still in a T-shirt, hiding from the killer, during a desert night where temperatures came close to -5°C (23°F)? And why were no man or dog tracks found at the scene of the hunt, which she claims went on for five hours? Then there is the question of Peter Falconio himself. Even given the size of the outback, it seems strange that aboriginal trackers and sniffer dogs never found his body. And why have ten independent witnesses come forward to say that they have seen Falconio alive since his disappearance?

IAN HUNTLEY

Ten-year-old Holly Wells and Jessica Chapman went for a walk on the evening of 4 August 2002 and disappeared. The chances that two apparently happy girls might choose to run away with no coats and no money seemed slim, but few liked to contemplate the obvious alternative – that they had been kidnapped.

The population of the girls' village, Soham in Cambridgeshire, rallied around their frightened families, and many locals helped the police search the surrounding countryside. A photograph of the smiling pair, taken just moments before they went on their fateful walk – dressed in bright red Manchester United football shirts – stared out from every news programme and national newspaper. However, over the following days, hopes of finding the children alive fell lower and lower.

Then, on 17 August, the police arrested two suspects: a man and a woman. The man led detectives to the bodies in the ditch where he had dumped them, just a few miles from Soham. The corpses had badly decomposed in the summer heat, and an attempt had been made to burn them.

To the shock of the village, the arrested pair was revealed to be Ian Huntley, aged 29, the caretaker at Jessica and Holly's primary school, and his girlfriend, Maxine Carr, aged 26, a classroom assistant at the same place. Maxine had worked with the girls and Huntley had been prominent among the good neighbours who had helped in the search for them. He had even given a short interview to a TV journalist, speaking of his hopes that they would be found alive.

Carr and Huntley went on trial in December 2003. To everyone's surprise, Huntley admitted killing the children, but

ABOVE Holly Wells and Jessica Chapman, photographed just a few minutes before they were murdered. The girls had been at a barbeque at Holly's house, and asked if they could walk to the local shop to buy sweets. On the way they were met by Ian Huntley...

BELOW Ian Huntley, pictured before his arrest, during a TV interview. He told the interviewer how worried he was about the missing girls – secretly knowing, of course, that they were both dead.

AN INSANITY PLEA?

Ian Huntley's ridiculously improbable explanation of the girls' deaths may have been a sly attempt to convince the court that he was mad. However, the report by psychiatrist Dr Christopher Clark scotched that possibility. Clark wrote: "Although Mr Huntley made clear attempts to appear insane, I have no doubt that the man currently, and at the time of the murders, was both physically and mentally sound and therefore, if he is found guilty, carried out the murders totally aware of his actions."

denied murdering them. He claimed that they had passed by his house on the evening of 4 August, and had come inside because Holly had a nosebleed. She had gone into his bathroom to wash her face and had somehow drowned in the bath – Huntley was vague about the details of just how such an accident could have befallen a healthy ten-year-old. He said Jessica had panicked when she saw that Holly was dead and, in covering her mouth to stifle her screams, he had accidentally smothered her to death. The fact that he would have had to cover her mouth and nose for at least three minutes in order to kill her (and she would inevitably have stopped screaming at an early stage of this happening) was left unexplained by Huntley.

Maxine Carr was not charged with involvement in the murders, mainly because she had been hundreds of miles away, in Grimsby, on the evening of the killings. She admitted lying to police to provide Huntley with an alibi, but insisted she had not believed him guilty until he confessed.

However, her insistence that she had covered up for Huntley because she wanted to start a family with him was somewhat shaken when it was revealed that she had been visiting her other lover, a 17-year-old rugby player, on the evening in question.

Huntley, unsurprisingly, was found guilty of double murder and sentenced to 40 years to life in prison. Maxine Carr was found guilty of perverting the course of justice, and was sentenced to three-and-a-half years.

Of course, the question remains as to what actually happened on that August evening in Ian Huntley's home. The autopsies made it clear that the girls had not been raped. It seems likely that Huntley meant to sexually proposition or abuse them as it later transpired that he had previously been accused of sexual misconduct with under-aged girls. However, the police had not passed on this information to the school authorities when he applied for the job of school caretaker. It is also extremely probable that he killed Holly and Jessica to prevent them telling anyone what he had attempted to do.

ABOVE Maxine Carr was a teaching assistant at Jessica and Holly's school – Jessica's mother later said that Maxine was her daughter's favourite member of staff. Although vilified by the newspapers, Carr's only real fault seems to have been that she trusted Huntley enough to provide him with a false alibi.

BELOW The bath in which Ian Huntley murdered Holly Wells. He claimed that she drowned accidentally, but it would have been next to impossible for a healthy girl to have died in such a small volume of water unless she had been held under the surface.

NEIL ENTWISTLE

Rachel Souza – an exchange student from Kingston, Massachusetts – met Neil Entwistle while they were both studying in the United Kingdom at York University. They married and, when she fell pregnant, the couple decided to move to Massachusetts to start a new life.

They settled in the prosperous town of Hopkinton, and Entwistle told his new neighbours that he was a successful internet entrepreneur. But his internet businesses were actually what a BBC journalist later called "get-rich-quick internet scams, pornographic websites and an online software company", none of which made any money. In reality, the 29-year-old was tens of thousands of dollars in debt.

Neither was he a devoted husband and family man… if he wasn't actually cheating on his wife with other women, it wasn't for want of trying. Police checks on his internet usage later showed that in the days leading up to the deaths of his wife and baby, he had been surfing adult dating and escort service websites. He had even exchanged e-mails with prospective dates, trying to arrange "discreet relationships". He had also been looking at websites that gave advice on bankruptcy, methods of suicide and how to kill other people.

It is still not clear exactly what happened on the evening of 20 January 2006 in the Entwistle home. The prosecution at Neil's subsequent trial suggested that the couple had argued over their debts or, possibly, Neil's internet philandering. What is clear is that 27-year-old Rachel was holding their nine-month-old daughter Lillian in her arms when a .22 bullet was fired from a Colt revolver, point-blank into the baby's stomach. The bullet passed through Lillian, killing her instantly, and lodged in Rachel's chest. Rachel was then killed by a shot to the forehead.

Entwistle claimed to have come home and found his wife and child already dead, but this statement was badly undermined by his actions in the immediate aftermath. Instead of ringing the emergency services or running to his neighbours for help, he booked himself onto a trans-Atlantic flight and flew to England that same night.

He was extradited back to the United States soon afterwards, but Entwistle's conviction remained far from certain as, without having any witnesses to the

ABOVE Rachel and Neil Entwistle with their baby, Lillian. Neil was seen, by friends and relatives, as a good husband and a doting father – indeed, his extravagant affection for little Lillian was described as "show-stopping."

BELOW A policeman holds up the Colt .22 "Diamondback" revolver that Entwistle used to murder his wife and daughter. The long, 15-cm (6-in) barrel was designed with target shooting in mind, which made it unwieldy for such a small calibre weapon.

THE PRICE OF PROTECTION

In August 2008 Entwistle – clearly an unpopular figure even among other imprisoned murderers – shaved his head in the hope of receiving protection from a "skinhead" white supremacist gang. They are reported to have told him: "It's a nice gesture on your part; but we're still gonna kill you."

ABOVE Neil Entwistle under arrest. The usual reason that fathers kill their own children is an acrimonious relationship break-up, when custody of the offspring seems likely to go to the mother. It is possible, therefore, that Rachel had threatened Neil with divorce.

BELOW The court is shown a photo the Entwistles' bed. The lump under the duvet was made by the corpses of Rachel and Lillian. Neil took a moment to cover them up, before hurrying to catch the next flight to the UK.

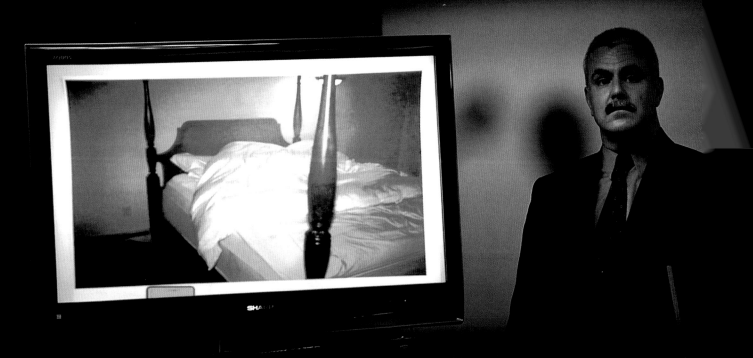

crime, the prosecution case was entirely circumstantial. His defence council insisted that the combined evidence of his massive debts, his dubious businesses, his internet dating and even his suspicious web search on the subject of "how to kill someone with a knife", did not add up to conclusive proof that he was guilty of murder and infanticide. They claimed that it was Rachel herself who was the murderer: she, they said, had tried to kill herself with a shot to the heart through the baby but when only Lillian died, Rachel shot herself in the forehead.

In fact it was the murder weapon that probably did the most to convince the jury that Neil Entwistle was guilty. Although it fired only small .22 bullets, the Colt Diamondback was a bulky gun with a very long barrel. It seemed ridiculous to suggest that a woman with a baby in one arm could have fired it first into the child and her own chest then, wounded, raise the clumsy weapon to shoot herself in the forehead.

The DNA report from the gun backed this up conclusively: Rachel's DNA was found only on the barrel and muzzle of the gun, while

Neil's was on the ammunition cylinder, the safety lock and the handgrip. This suggested that Rachel had grabbed the gun as Neil raised it after shooting the baby, but he had forced it against her head and pulled the trigger.

Neil Entwistle was found guilty of double homicide on 26 June 2008. Massachusetts has no death penalty, but it does have a mandatory sentence for convicted murderers of life imprisonment with no chance of parole. Neil Entwistle was given two of these sentences: one for the killing of his wife and the other for the murder of their baby.

PEDRO LOPEZ

In April 1980, the rain-swollen river flowing through the Ecuadorian town of Ambato overflowed its banks and revealed the part-buried bodies of four missing prepubescent girls. A few days later, the man who became known as the "Monster of the Andes" tried to lure away the 11-year-old daughter of Carlina Ramon Poveda. Luckily the frantic mother caught up with her child, who was walking hand in hand with her abductor. Poveda denounced him and summoned some local men to help her. They held him down until the police arrived.

LEFT The Ecuadorian hill town of Ambato, where Lopez was eventually caught. The remoteness of many Andean towns, and the failure of communication between different police jurisdictions, allowed Lopez to escape justice for a decade.

The prisoner, 31-year-old Pedro Alonzo Lopez, denied that he had anything to do with the murders. But a priest who posed as a fellow prisoner finally talked him into bragging a confession. Confronted with his own words, Lopez decided to open the floodgates: he told police that over the past decade he had raped and killed about 360 little girls (an average of three murders a month). If true, that made Lopez the most prolific living serial killer on record.

Lopez later told the story of his life to American journalist Ron Laytner. Born in Tolima, Colombia, the seventh son of a prostitute, Lopez was thrown out of the house by his mother at the age of eight. The boy was raped by a stranger, and then drifted to the city of Bogotá where he begged in the streets for ten years. At the age of 18, in prison for stealing a car, he was gang-raped by four other prisoners. It took him two weeks to manufacture a knife; then he lured the rapists, one by one, into a dark cell and killed three of them. The fourth managed to escape.

Released from prison in 1969, Lopez began raping and murdering young girls, preferably under the age of 12. His victims were mostly native children, as the authorities did not pay much attention to their disappearance.

Lopez's method was always the same: to walk around a Columbian or Ecuadorian town market until he saw a girl with "a certain look of innocence and beauty". He would follow the girl – if necessary, for days – until her mother left her alone. When it was safe he would approach the girl and tell her that he had a present for her mother, and then he would lead her by the hand to the outskirts of the town.

If night fell, he would forcibly keep the child with him, trying to soothe her with promises and gentle words. But, as soon

BELOW A homeless child sleeps on the street in the exclusive Copacabana borough of Brazil's Rio de Janeiro. Such children are sometimes murdered by "death squads" – thugs paid to "clean up the area" by those with an interest in maintaining the tourist trade.

ABOVE Pedro Lopez, pictured after his arrest in 1980. Arguably most dangerous serial killer on record, Lopez is – thanks to the Ecuadorian authorities – presently free and his whereabouts are unknown.

OUR GLOBAL SHAME

The United Nation's International Children's Emergency Fund (UNICEF) believes that there are 100 million "street children" living outdoors and unprotected around the world. Over 11 million live in India alone, and between 750,000 and a million are thought to be living on the streets in the USA. Many such children never reach adulthood. It is likely that Pedro Lopez's brutal ten years as a street child, during which he was raped at least once, had a strong influence in turning him into a serial killer.

as the sun had risen, he would rape and simultaneously strangle her. He would only kill the children in daylight, he later said, because he wanted to see the life drain from their eyes.

Asked to explain how he justified his murders, Lopez told Laytner: "The arrival of life is divine. It comes through the act of sex. And so if an innocent person dies in the act of sex, it is also divine. That person will find heaven without suffering in this world."

Lopez later lowered his claim to 140 murders. It is not known if this reappraisal contributed to the prison authorities' decision to free him, on grounds of good conduct, in early 1999. This model behaviour did not, however, prevent the Ecuadorian government immediately deporting him to Colombia.

Political relations between Ecuador and Columbia have been very bad for a number of years. Instead of handing Lopez over to the Colombian authorities to stand trial for his crimes in that country, the Ecuadorians are said to have simply taken Lopez at night over the Columbian border and secretly released him.

Lopez is on record as saying that, if freed, he would return to his "mission" to rape and kill little girls. Even Victor Lascano, the governor of the Ambato Prison that held Lopez for nearly 20 years, is quoted as saying of the release: "God save the children. He is unreformed and totally remorseless. This whole nightmare may start again." Pedro Lopez's present whereabouts are unknown.

HAROLD SHIPMAN

n the autumn of 1998, police arrested a Manchester GP, Dr Harold Frederick Shipman, on suspicion of murder. At the time even the investigators found it hard to convince themselves that this pleasant mannered man, with a practice of over 3,000 patients, could be a killer. But as the evidence mounted, they began to suspect that he was actually the most ruthless killer in British legal history.

B orn in Nottingham, Shipman had struggled out of his working-class background to win a place at Leeds University Medical School. Sadly, he was a less than brilliant student and had a rather distant manner. Yet, despite these inadequacies, he had a pompously high opinion of himself, and behaved like a ruthless bully to anyone who didn't dare stand up to him. If a receptionist forgot his coffee, for example, he would go white with rage; a typical reaction was the occasion when his quiet wife Primrose rang him to say that she and the children were hungry and waiting to eat dinner. He was heard to snap coldly: "You'll wait until I get there!"

Shipman's early career was marred by the discovery that he was addicted to pethidine (a medical morphine derivative), which he had been stealing by forging prescriptions. He was fined and temporarily suspended from practising medicine, an event that seems to have made him deeply bitter.

ABOVE A newspaper signboard outside Shipman's former GP surgery in Hyde, Manchester. Shipman's suicide was reported with delight by most newspapers, but it would have been better if he had lived to confess, and thus give us insights into preventing similar serial murders in the future.

RIGHT Primrose Shipman, the wife of "Doctor Death". There is no evidence that Primrose knew about Shipman's many murders, and she still says that she believes in his innocence.

DOCUMENTS

ITEM 5
The death certificate of Kathleen Grundy, the former Mayor of Hyde, signed by Shipman and giving the (false) cause of death as "Old Age". Grundy was the last of Shipman's victims, all of whom were murdered under a cloak of medical officialdom and red tape.

ITEM 6
A witness statement, made by Angela Woodruff, the daughter of Kathleen Grundy. It was this statement that eventually led to Harold Shipman's downfall. It is very likely that Dr Shipman would have continued to kill, if police had not acted on Mrs Woodruff's suspicions.

ITEM 7
In this handwritten note given to his trial judge, serial killer Michel Fourniret admits to being a "bad [human] being devoid of all human sentiment". He adds: "the cupboard of my conscience, wide open, is empty". This letter was his only public statement, as he refused to speak in court. (See over for translation).

ITEM 8
A suspect sketch of Marc Dutroux, the paedophile and murderer, whose crimes shook Belgium to the core. His own mother is quoted as saying of him: "What I do not know, and what all the people who know him fear, it's what he has in mind for the future."

None of the people really concerned in this trial can expect to come out of it unscathed. It is them, and them alone, whom I wish to address.

PREFACE

Difficult for me to speak when anything there is to say is no better than silence.

But, the right to remain silent is not given to somebody who, having had to take the decision to boycott the trial, owed it to himself to come and expound the reasons that have left him with no choice.

INTRODUCTION
PUBLIC HEARING

The public hearing of this trial would involve all the participants lending themselves to a theatricality that mocks the dignity of the families of the direct victims, the indirect victims of my actions.

In particular:

The presence of an audience of X times more gawpers and idlers of all kinds than people involved inevitably muzzles the guilty party which I am, that is an evil being devoid of all human sentiment.

1. As a first consequence of which, I owed it to myself to come here to confirm the position that I have expounded to my lawyers ever since the morning of the extradition.

A position that I have not ceased to hammer home to all the various interlocutors from the Judicial City. Especially all the experts in the art of listening who comprise the team of investigating officers in the enquiries and the other examinations made with a fine-tooth comb all over the place without respite, justified by matters here and there that have still not been elucidated, in Europe and elsewhere.

This position, expounded many times, has six words:

"TRIAL WITHOUT CLOSED HEARING = LIPS SEALED"

This position will undoubtedly appear unusual, in the face of the routine functioning of a judicial machine more prone to obey reactive reflexes than analytical sagacity.

Nevertheless, unusual or otherwise, the position of silence in the absence of a closed hearing, followed by the decision to boycott the trial, were weighed up and mulled over for a long time.

2. As a second consequence of the absence of a closed hearing, I owed it to myself to come here to confirm verbally to the families my very ardent hope to meet them. I think there is no match for the contents exchanged in a tête-à-tête dialogue. Such a meeting is dear to me, I am merely coming here to confirm the offer made to your lawyers, Madame and Monsieur, via the unambiguous terms of my letter of the seventh of July 2007.

My proposal of a tête-à-tête! This is nothing more than a barricade erected against the consequences of various forms of delirium. I do not have the right, as long as my body carries me, to not fight, to not take up arms against that which leads the families to all types of suppositions and pursues them in their insomnia.

What I see in a tête-à-tête is the fundamental importance of the current of spontaneous sincerity proper to the absolute nature of a face-to-face meeting, eye to eye.

I leave it to other people to believe that it is possible to have the same person-to-person relationship in public as in private.

The fact that I consider the only meeting I shall have with the families in my lifetime of capital importance leaves me no choice but to say to them:

"Do the impossible to be able to come and spit in my face, it is the least I owe you!"

Up until the last few days, I made the mistake of thinking that, although most of the cases will barely acquire any further clarification through such interviews, this is far from true of the BRICHET, BOUZET and SAISON families.

My regret, not to say my resentment at my late awakening, is that the obvious primacy of direct contact over contact via intermediaries, interpreters and other substituting actors only became apparent to me in the presence of Monsieur NAVILLE, in the Place de Saint Cyr les Colons.

A meeting without the influence of which my communication of a flow of information and suggestions to the squad of gendarmes with their notebooks in their hands, to the Auxerre brigade making good use of the absence of "civilians", at midday, a time suited to the most productive briefings, would never have taken place.

There is a fine, good quality to the direct face-to-face that allowed the localization work in the Othe Forest to be completed, in accordance with my statements, despite the people who became sceptical after the procedures of the "interrogation of the records" by the gendarmes of DIJON proved to be in vain.

3. If it was only a question of chopping off my head, the narcissistic manipulator that some people, virtuosos in the subject, see in me could only be flattered by the privilege of being ritually offered up for collective condemnation. But, once it has been chopped off, my head would discover the benefits of tranquility.

Finally, I shall not lie, by closing to add that, although M.O. is no more perfect than many of her fellow creatures, never never did this poor misfit, to my knowledge, contrary to what the local 7pm television news of 24 March saw fit to announce, become a kind of agony aunt Machiavellianly conceived to sell parts of paradise, after the advertisement of one of those convicts who receives no mail or is on the lookout for any opportunity to escape at the least cost!

No! She fell inexorably into the hateful clutches of a perverse manipulator! Of a manipulator perverse enough to seek to exploit without the least shame the stupor and naïve candour of isolated or suffering people. A filthy guy who, under the insidious cover of anonymity, never had any other aim than the domination and enslavement of elderly or hospitalized people whose letter box never receives anything more than brochures or bills.

A filthy abuser of trust who, driven at most by the narcissistic desire to give himself a good conscience while passing the time, made known via the Catholic press* the existence of the network of friendship and voluntary work.

* and also via the broadcast "Coeurs Pyramide" by Patricia DOUART, on RADIO TROIS.

Without a closed hearing; not a word!

By 1977 Shipman had joined the Donnybrook House GP practice in Hyde, Greater Manchester, where he eventually became a senior partner. In 1997, Dr Linda Reynolds noticed that Shipman seemed to have been present at the deaths of three times as many patients as might have been statistically expected. She passed on her suspicions to the local coroner, but her report was not followed up.

Shipman came under official scrutiny after the sudden death of an elderly patient, Kathleen Grundy, on 24 June 1998. Mrs Grundy had apparently left a will in which her considerable fortune – over £300,000 – was left to her doctor, Harold Shipman. The will was carelessly typed, and the two witnesses who had acted as signatories later explained that they had done so as a favour to Dr Shipman, and that he had folded the paper so they could not see what they were signing.

But it was not until September 1998, when Mrs Grundy's body was exhumed, that the authorities felt there was enough evidence to arrest Dr Shipman. The post-mortem clearly showed that Mrs Grundy had died of an overdose of injected morphine. After that, another 14 exhumations of Shipman's patients revealed the same cause of death. Moreover, it was clear that these 15 were only a small proportion of those he had murdered.

At first Dr Shipman appeared full of self-confidence when the police confronted him

with these discoveries. But then a detective constable pointed out that he had made extensive changes to his patients' records – often just minutes after their deaths – to make them seem more ill than they had actually been. (Shipman was evidently unaware that the computer automatically registered the date and time of every one of these changes.) This threw him badly and he began to falter and flounder. That evening he broke down and sobbed.

Yet there was no confession. From that moment onward, he simply refused to co-operate during interviews, frequently

sitting with his back to the interviewer and remaining silent.

Following his conviction, Shipman was given 15 life sentences for murdering 15 of his elderly patients by injecting them with lethal doses of diamorphine (medical heroine). A government report later concluded that he had possibly murdered between 215 and 260 people over his 23-year period in general practice.

Shipman was found hanged in his cell on the morning of 13 January 2004. Self-righteous to the end, he never admitted any of the murders.

A PLACID KILLER

Unlike most serial killers, there seems to have been no sexual or sadistic element to Doctor Shipman's murders. He killed most of his victims in their own homes, convincing them that he was giving them a normal, harmless drug injection. But these were definitely *not* mercy killings: although all his known victims were elderly, few were actually seriously ill or even in particular discomfort. Given his egotistical character, it seems likely that Shipman simply became addicted to the god-like power of handing out death.

TOP Harold Shipman at the time of his arrest. As a teenager he watched his mother slowly die of cancer, her pain only eased by a doctor's injections of morphine. Was Shipman masochistically re-enacting his mother's death with each murder?

ABOVE Some of Harold Shipman's known victims. From top left: Norah Nuttall, Jean Lilley, Marie West, Irene Turner, Lizzie Adams, Winifred Mellor, Kathleen Grundy, Joan Melia, Bianka Pomfret, Maureen Ward, Kathleen Wagstaff and Pamela Hillier.

MICHEL FOURNIRET AND MONIQUE OLIVIER

Michel Fourniret first came into contact with Monique Olivier in 1986 through an advertisement seeking a pen pal he had placed in a religious magazine. At the time he was not in a position to offer any greater intimacy, as he was serving a prison sentence for sexual assault. The 44-year-old French forest warden was cautious in explaining his circumstances, but things went so well in their correspondence that he eventually admitted his obsession with virgin girls… and how much he wanted to rape and kill them.

Monique apparently remained impassive, admitting that she herself daydreamed about murdering her ex-husband. Letters found later by the police showed that the pair entered a written pact: Michel would kill Monique's ex (the one murder, in fact, that he never carried out) provided she helped him to hunt down young women and girls.

Monique and Michel got together as soon as he was released from jail. They bought an isolated chateau in the Ardennes region of eastern France, and from there they went on lengthy trips in their van – sometimes right across France or over the border into Belgium – hunting for vulnerable girls who looked like they might be virgins.

Their first known victim was Isabelle Lavel. The 17-year-old was walking home from school in Auxerre on 11 December 1987, when Fourniret and Olivier stopped in their small van and asked her for directions. Since they were a couple she most likely felt safe enough when they asked her to climb in and show them the way in person. Her skeleton was found at the bottom of a local well 19 years later.

Over the next three years, Fourniret kidnapped and murdered at least four more young women: Fabienne Leroy, aged 20; Jeanne-Marie Desramault, aged 22; Elisabeth Brichet, aged 12 and 13-year-old Natacha Danais. Monique Olivier was instrumental in the kidnappings, lulling the girls into a false sense of security, but it was usually Fourniret who assaulted and killed the girls.

Fourniret then murdered Farida Hellegouarch, the wife of his former cellmate, the bank robber Jean-Pierre Hellegouarch. Fourniret had guessed that Farida knew the location of some hidden bank loot and, so in 1990 he kidnapped her, forced her to reveal its location and then killed her. Shortly after Farida's disappearance, Fourniret and Olivier could suddenly afford to pay off the mortgage on their chateau in full.

There followed an apparent ten-year break in which they refrained from murder, but on 16 May 2000, Céline Saison from Charleville was killed. The following year, Manyana Thumpong, aged 13, was kidnapped, raped and murdered. Lastly, Fourniret killed an as yet unidentified man in the course of robbing him.

ABOVE LEFT 12-year-old Elisabeth Brichet; kidnapped, raped and murdered by Fourniret in 1989. Elisabeth's disappearance was falsely attributed to Marc Dutroux (see page 38) until Fourniret confessed and led police to her buried corpse.

ABOVE RIGHT Fourniret and Olivier's home – Sautou Chateau near Donchery the French Ardenne – is searched for bodies by the police. Nicknamed the "Ogre of Ardennes", Fourniret confessed to nine killings, but is suspected of being responsible for another ten.

ABOVE The two handguns found at Chateau Sautou by police. Fourniret is a classic example of how a sex abuser can further deteriorate into a rapist and serial killer. The need to dominate victims can be a downward spiral into violence and murder.

BELOW Monique Olivier and Michel Fourniret pictured in 1992 when they were still at large. Born in 1950, Olivier will be at least 86 years old before she has a chance to see freedom. Fourniret, born in 1942, will die in prison.

At last Michel and Monique's run of luck came to an end. On 26 June 2003, Fourniret abducted a 13-year-old girl from near the village of Ciney. He tied her up and dumped her in the back of his van. However, she managed to bite through the ropes and escaped... but not before she had memorized the licence plate of the van.

The couple were arrested and – terrified by the possibility that she might spend the rest of her life in jail – Monique confessed, insisting that she had been forced by Fourniret to help kidnap his victims. However, during the trial the letters mentioning their murder pact were produced and her defence fell apart. In May 2008, Monique Olivier was found guilty of direct involvement in one murder

and of aiding another six murders. She was sentenced to 28 years to life in prison.

Michel Fourniret himself confessed immediately after his arrest – admitting to the kidnappings, the rapes and to killing victims with a gun, by strangulation and by stabbing with a screwdriver. He was convicted of seven of his nine confessed killings and sentenced to life imprisonment without remission.

MADAME MURDERER

Certain facts about Monique Olivier horrified the court: for example, she admitted that she and Fourniret would re-enact the rape and murder of his victims to spice up their sex life. And then there was the evidence that they had taken their baby son, born in 1988, on their "hunting trips" to further lull potential victims into a false sense of security. But it was the fact that she had kept silent about the murders for over 16 years and had in some cases sat in the van listening while Fourniret committed rape and murder that seems to have guaranteed Olivier at least 28 years in prison.

JOHN BUNTING

The discovery of Australia's worst known case of serial killing took place in Snowtown, a tiny place with fewer than 1,000 inhabitants, about 161 kilometres (100 miles) north of the city of Adelaide. On 20 May 1999, police investigating a series of local disappearances searched a derelict building – a former bank – in the centre of Snowtown and found six black plastic barrels in the abandoned vault. The barrels contained the remains of eight corpses, some dismembered.

The following day, investigating officers arrested three men in the northern suburbs of Adelaide: John Justin Bunting, aged 32; Robert Joe Wagner, aged 27, and Mark Ray Haydon, aged 40. A few days later they also arrested James Spyridon Vlassakis, aged 19. Excavation in Bunting's garden uncovered two more corpses.

As the investigation and identification of the victims progressed, a bizarre story emerged. The ringleader of the killers was Bunting, a small but powerful abattoir worker who had decided to murder anyone he suspected of being a paedophile. To do this, he felt he needed accomplices.

Robert Wagner was both Bunting's contact with the paedophile underworld and his right-hand man in most of the killings. One of Bunting's first victims was a man who had sexually abused Wagner: convicted paedophile Barry Lane. Using information gleaned from Wagner and Lane, Bunting set about designing what he called his "spider wall" – a collection of names connected by pieces of string to indicate who knew whom. Bunting used this to plot his murders.

James Vlassakis had fallen under the older man's spell when his mother had an affair with Bunting. Several years later, Vlassakis was involved in three of the killings, including that of his own half-brother – Troy Youde – whom Vlassakis had accused of sexually molesting him.

Bunting "punished" his victims, torturing them with a variety of gruesome implements, including ropes and electrical tape, knives, saws, a shotgun, pliers, lit cigars, a welding machine that could administer powerful electric shocks and, in one case, a lighted sparkler forced up a victim's penis. But this wasn't justice – it was sadism of the darkest kind. Indeed, most of his victims were plainly not paedophiles. The likely truth is that Bunting was addicted to torture and murder, and targeted those he thought society would not care about or miss. His accomplices seem

ABOVE A police backhoe excavates the garden at Waterloo Corner Road, North Salisbury, in Adelaide. The "Snowtown murders" proved to be Australia's worst known case of serial crime to date.

to have been drawn into his spider web of homicide through his powerful personality and the fear that they might be next on his list. And by involving them in the killings, Bunting effectively removed any chance that they might go to the police.

Perhaps the most surprising of Bunting's confederates was Mark Haydon. In November 1998, Bunting killed Elizabeth Haydon: Mark's wife and mother of his two small children. Bunting had two reasons for murdering Elizabeth – she had outraged his moral sensibilities when she had admitted to being attracted to him… and she was obese. Bunting strangled her while Mark Haydon was out of the house, but admitted the crime when the unsuspecting widower arrived home. Haydon had already been involved in covering up one of the previous murders, and apparently reacted to the killing of his wife with equanimity. The two men dumped her body in a barrel full of acid and remained friends.

Tried in September 2003, Bunting was convicted of 11 murders. Although 12 bodies were connected to the case, the jury felt that one woman – Bunting's lover Suzanne Allan – might, as he claimed, have died from a heart attack and that he had merely dismembered her and buried her corpse in the garden. Wagner was convicted of being involved in ten of the murders. Both were given life sentences with no chance of parole. Vlassakis pleaded guilty to involvement in three murders and was given 26 years. Mark Haydon admitted to assisting after the fact in two murders – that of his wife and of Troy Youde – and was sentenced to 25 years.

ABOVE Reporters view the cavity from which the police removed two bodies from John Bunting's garden. While most serial killers hunt victims on their own – or, at most, with a single "partner" – Bunting gathered a whole gang to help him kill.

NASTY TOURISTS

The long-term impact of the killings on Snowtown was grim. Residents of the tiny hamlet even considered changing the municipality's name in the hope of putting off the steady stream of ghoulish sightseers who wished to see (and smell) the vault that had contained the half-dissolved bodies.

LEFT John Bunting (left) and Robert Wagner (right) under arrest. As the ringleader, Bunting was responsible for targeting victims and for much of the torture, but Wagner was a willing helper.

RIGHT The abandoned bank building in Snowtown, where Bunting and his confederates hid the remains of eight of their victims. The new owner of the building has said that they want to turn it into a bed-and-breakfast establishment.

FRED AND ROSE WEST

In the summer of 1993, Frederick and Rosemary West – a builder and his wife living at 25 Cromwell Street in Gloucester – were accused of sexually assaulting a young woman. The charges were eventually dropped, but in the meantime the West children had been taken into care. It was during this period that foster-carers overheard them talking about their older sister Heather being "under the patio". When questioned about this ominous-sounding phrase, the children said that they had been told she had been working in the Midlands for the past five years, but that their parents would still occasionally threaten them with being "put under the patio with Heather".

The police checked the records against Heather West's National Insurance number, and became suspicious when they found that she had never claimed any state benefits or National Health care. They applied for a warrant and entered 25 Cromwell Street to dig up the patio. When they found the dismembered skeleton of a young girl, Fred West was arrested.

He admitted to killing 16-year-old Heather in 1987, but insisted his wife Rose knew nothing about it. As West refused to confess to anything else, the investigation might have rested there, but then the scene-of-crime

officers unearthed a third femur: evidently there was more than one body at the Cromwell Street address.

Further excavations unearthed the remains of eight more victims beneath the patio, cellar and bathroom. Under intense interrogation, Fred admitted to these killings, plus a further three murders. He had buried the other bodies out in the Gloucestershire countryside.

Fred's first known victim was Anna McFall in 1967 – she was pregnant with his baby and was pressuring him to marry her. After killing her, he carefully dismembered her body and buried it along with the

ABOVE The cellar at 25 Cromwell Street where five dismembered corpses were found. West had buried the bodies in a pattern that formed a circle. They had been placed clockwise in the order they were killed, but why Fred West did this we will probably never be known.

TOP The exterior of 25 Cromwell Street during the police investigation. After Rose West was convicted the house was torn down by Gloucester County Council, partly to prevent it becoming a ghoulish tourist attraction.

ABOVE The ten known victims of Fred and Rose West. Although Fred confessed to these killings, it seems likely that he withheld information on other murders. Certainly there are a number of unsolved missing person cases from around Gloucester that might be the result of Fred's serial killing spree.

RIGHT Fred and Rosemarie West. It has been suggested that Fred became homicidal after suffering several injuries to his head in his youth – lacerations to the prefrontal lobes of the brain have been linked to both sexual hyperactivity and violent behaviour. Rose, however, just seems to have followed Fred's lead.

foetus in a field. He kept her fingers and toes, however, treasuring them as a keepsake.

In the summer of 1971, Fred was living with 18-year-old Rosemarie Letts (soon to become Mrs Rose West). It was during this time that he apparently killed eight-year-old Charmaine, his estranged wife Rena's daughter from a previous relationship. At the time Fred had custody of both Charmaine and Anne-Marie – his own daughter with Rena – and it took a few months for his wife to ask where her eldest child was. When it became obvious that Rena might go to the authorities, Fred got her drunk, strangled and dismembered her, then buried the body parts under his house.

In 1972, he killed Linda Gough, aged 21, and Lucy Partington, also aged 21 – burying them beneath 25 Cromwell Street. The following year he killed Carol Cooper, aged 15. In 1975, he killed Juanita Mott, aged 19, and Shirley Hubbard, aged 15. West killed no one (that we know of) in 1976, but in 1977 he murdered Therese Siegenthaler, aged 21, and Alison Chambers, aged 17. In 1978, he killed Shirley Robinson, aged 18, a lodger and lover who was heavily pregnant with Fred's baby. He then claimed to have given up murder until May 1987, when he killed

his eldest daughter Heather during an argument.

Fred West hanged himself in his cell on New Year's Day, 1995, before he could be tried; but the horror was not yet over. As the police investigation continued, it became increasingly clear that Fred's insistence that his wife Rose had known nothing about the murders was a lie.

Evidence given by the six surviving West children, and by friends and acquaintances, clearly indicated that Rose was fully involved in Fred's sexual predations. Further evidence came from a former beauty queen, Caroline Raine, who reported being abducted and sexually assaulted by both Fred and Rose West.

Then there was the circumstantial, yet damning, fact that eight-year-old Charmaine – the daughter of Fred's first wife, Rena – had been killed while Fred was in prison for petty theft. The most likely candidate for that murder was his then live-in lover Rose.

At the trial, held in October 1995, the prosecution claimed that Rose had helped in all ten of the killings that had taken place since 1972. The jury agreed (although there remains some doubt as to whether Rose actually helped kill her daughter Heather). She was sentenced to ten life terms in jail.

DARK SECRETS

When Rose's father once tried to persuade her to leave Fred, he noticed that a seemingly innocuous phrase from Fred clearly upset Rose terribly. Fred had implored Rose to stay with the words: "Come on, Rosie, you know what we've got between us."

MARC DUTROUX

On 28 May 1996, a 12-year-old Belgian girl, Sabine Dardenne, disappeared on her way to school. Two men, Michel Lelièvre and Marc Dutroux, had grabbed her and pulled her into a car. She was driven to a house belonging to Dutroux, where she was chained to a bed for three days. Then she was taken down to a homemade dungeon in the cellar and locked in. Over the next 80 days Sabine was repeatedly raped and underwent psychological torture by Dutroux.

She later told police that Dutroux had tried to convince her that he was protecting her from a gang of felons who had demanded money from her parents. When she tried to resist his sexual assaults, he threatened to hand her over to these men who, she said, "...would torture me and kill me after making me suffer."

After nearly three months underground, Sabine Dardenne was joined by another girl, 14-year-old Laetitia Delhez. A week later, however, both were rescued when police raided the house. It might have been hoped that Dutroux's arrest – along with Michel Lelièvre and Dutroux's wife Michelle – would have ended the horror, but much worse was to come.

Police searched another house belonging to Dutroux, but failed to find Julie Lejeune and Mélissa Russo, both aged nine, who were imprisoned in another hidden dungeon. Officers heard their plaintive cries for help, but thought the voices came from children playing in the street outside. The girls had been kidnapped on 24 June 1995, and had endured over a year of subterranean incarceration and sexual torture. They starved to death before another search revealed their location.

Marc Dutroux made no effort to warn the authorities that the girls were there. His wife Michelle later admitted that she knew the little girls were trapped and were starving to death. Although free on bail at that time, she did nothing to save them because, she said, she had been afraid they might attack her if she took them any food.

Also found in the second house was the corpse of Bernard Weinstein, Dutroux's lodger. He had killed Weinstein by crushing his testicles – torturing him to find out the hiding place of a cache of money.

Further searches of one of the basement dungeons unearthed the corpses of Eefje Lambrecks, aged 17, and An Marchal, 19. Both had been kidnapped while camping near Ostend on 22 August 1995. After three weeks of sexual abuse they had been strangled.

Public fury soon turned to suspicion. People asked just how Dutroux, an unemployed electrician, could have afforded to buy several houses and expensive cars. Why had he been released ten years early from prison – after a conviction for paedophilia – when he plainly had not been rehabilitated? And why did it take so long for him to be arrested in the face of mounting evidence that he might be connected to child disappearances?

Rumours of a paedophile gang, protected by members high up in the Belgian government and police force, shook the nation. In October 1996, 275,000 Belgians

TOP Marc Dutroux. In April 1998, Dutroux managed to escape while being transported to a court hearing. His jailors had failed to handcuff him and let him get hold of one of their handguns. Fortunately he was recaptured within a few hours.

ABOVE LEFT AND RIGHT: Mélissa Russo and Julie Lejeune, both aged eight. The girls were kidnapped together from Grâce-Hollogne on 24 June 1995. They endured almost six months of sexual abuse before they eventually starved to death in their hidden prison.

FRIENDS IN HIGH PLACES?

It seems odd that the jury and the three judges added a caveat to Marc Dutroux's sentence: that, should the authorities (again, inexplicably) decide to give him early parole, the government of the day has the right to add a further ten years onto his sentence to prevent his immediate release. The question is, why did they feel that this safety valve was necessary?

ABOVE Belgian police turn the grounds of one of Marc Dutroux's houses into a mud pit in their search for evidence. It has still not been fully explained just how Dutroux could afford so many houses. Was he indeed procuring little girls for rich and powerful paedophiles, as he claimed?

BELOW The interior of one of Marc Dutroux's houses. Dutroux made videos of his sexual abuse of his victims. The lodger he murdered, Bernard Weinstein, slept in a room scattered with these videos, so may well have been aware of Dutroux's activities.

joined a march through Brussels protesting against police incompetence over the Dutroux case and apparent government inactivity over paedophilia.

Marc Dutroux did not deny his kidnapping and paedophilia, but insisted he was merely a courier for a paedophile gang and it was they, not him, who had strangled the two girls found buried in his cellar. His "confession" implicated his wife Michelle, Michel Lelièvre (the man who had helped him kidnap Sabine Dardenne), and Michel Nihoul, a businessman who had helped Dutroux sell drugs; but Dutroux refused to name the other members of the claimed paedophile ring, other than to hint that at least two policemen were involved.

Marc Dutroux was sentenced to life imprisonment for kidnapping, rape and murder. His wife Michelle Martin was given 30 years for kidnapping and rape. Michel Lelièvre was given 25 years for kidnapping and drug dealing. Michel Nihoul was sentenced to five years for drug dealing and several counts of fraud.

AILEEN WUORNOS

Just 12 days before Christmas 1989, a body was found outside Ormond Beach, Florida, wrapped in an old carpet. The police identified the victim as Richard Mallory, a 51-year-old electrician with a previous conviction for rape. The autopsy showed that he had been shot four times with a .22 calibre handgun.

Over the next 12 months, five more victims were discovered in different locations but in almost identical circumstances: a 43-year-old construction worker, David Spears, shot six times with a .22 handgun; rodeo worker Charles Carskaddon, aged 40, with nine bullets in him; a 50-year-old truck driver called Troy Burress was killed by two .22 calibre bullets; a 56-year-old child abuse investigator, Charles Humphreys, was found shot six times in the torso and once in the head; and finally, on 19 November, the body of Walter Gino Antonio was discovered, murdered with four .22 calibre bullets.

In every case, money, valuables and the victim's vehicle had been stolen. Used condoms were also found at most of the crime scenes. Since the same handgun was being used in each of the murders, the police realized they had a serial killer on their hands. The FBI's psychological profiling unit concluded that this was probably a woman.

On 4 July 1990, the killer and her girlfriend skidded off the road in a car she had stolen from Peter Seims, a 65-year-old part-time missionary she had murdered in early June. Witnesses told the police that they had seen the two women – one tall and blonde, the other a short, heavy-set brunette – abandon

the damaged Pontiac Sunbird after removing the licence plates.

By December 1990, the police had two names to attach to artist's sketches of the women. The brunette was possibly one Tyria J Moore, a 28-year-old occasional hotel maid; and the blonde her live-in lover, a 34-year-old prostitute who went under several names, one of them being Lee Wuornos.

On 9 January 1991, the police arrested Wuornos outside The Last Resort bikers' bar in Volusia County, Florida. Shortly afterwards, Tyria Moore was located at her sister's home in Pennsylvania but was not arrested. Moore, who admitted that Wuornos had told her about

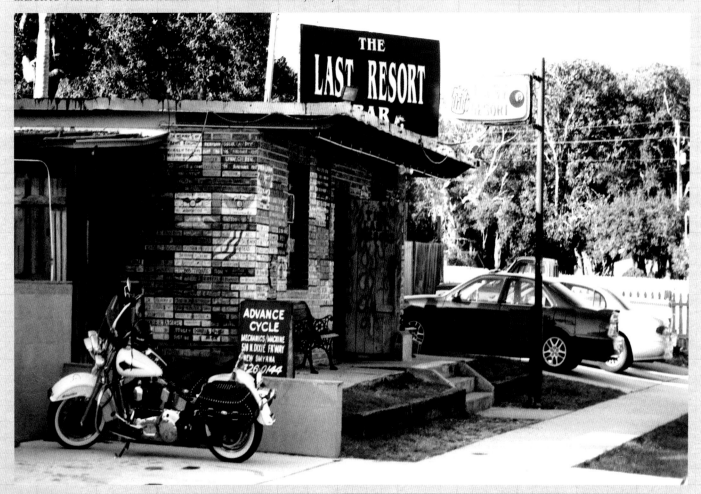

ABOVE The Last Resort biker bar. Wuornos made her money as a highway prostitute – a highly dangerous profession for a woman working on her own. As a result she spent a lot of her spare time getting drunk in bars.

ABOVE LEFT Victim Peter Seims, aged 65, killed by Wuornos around the beginning of June 1990. His body has never been found, but his car led to his killer's downfall. Wuornos and Moore crashed it during a joyride and police found a partial palm print on the abandoned vehicle.

ABOVE RIGHT Tyria Moore, Wuornos's lover, gives evidence for the prosecution at one of Aileen's trials. It was Moore's persuasion that caused Wuornos to confess.

BELOW Wuornos had a difficult childhood: abandoned by her parents, she later claimed that she was sexually molested by the grandfather she lived with. She gave birth, after being raped, at 14, and had the child adopted. At 15 her grandfather threw her out to fend for herself.

at least one of the murders, agreed to help the prosecution in return for immunity from the charge of "accessory after the fact". She led officers to the creek where Wuornos had thrown the .22 revolver used in the murders. Then, under police supervision, she made 11 bugged phone calls to Wuornos in prison, claiming that she remained undiscovered by the police and urging Wuornos to confess. Wuornos, who was plainly still in love with Moore, tried to calm her and agreed to make a statement.

On 16 January 1991, Wuornos gave a three-hour videotaped confession. In it she admitted to killing all seven men. She also provided details that only a witness to the murders could have known, apparently confirming her testimony. Defending the killings, she insisted that she had only gone to the woods with them to trade sex for money. Each of the seven men had tried to attack or rape her, she said, forcing her to kill them in self-defence. But would even a hardworking street prostitute need to kill seven men in the space of a single year?

Initially tried for only the murder of Richard Mallory, the jury found Wuornos guilty and she was sentenced to death in the electric chair. At a subsequent arraignment for three of the other murders, Lee (real name Aileen) Wuornos pleaded guilty and requested the death sentence without trial on the grounds that she wanted to "be with Jesus". Yet she became enraged when the judge complied with her request, shouting that she was being executed for being a rape victim. As she was led out of the courtroom, Wuornos yelled that she hoped that the judge's wife and children might be raped too.

Aileen Wuornos was executed by lethal injection on 9 October 2002.

HELL'S ANGEL

The controlling emotion of Aileen Wuornos's life seems to have been embittered fury. As she was led out of the court, following her first conviction and death sentence in 1991, she shouted: "I'm going to Heaven now. You're all going to Hell!" Shortly after her death, an anonymous joker posted a message on a website that was hosting an online discussion about her execution. Signed "Satan", it simply read: "Umm… could you guys take her back?"

ROBERT "WILLIE" PICKTON

The city of Vancouver, British Columbia, is a lovely town. Surrounded by beautiful snow-capped mountains, it has a thriving movie-making industry and cultural life. Indeed, it has been ranked for over a decade by the *Economist* magazine as one of the world's most "liveable cities". But Vancouver has a dark side – the run-down, crime-ridden Downtown Eastside district – stalked for almost two decades by a homicidal monster.

Perhaps it was actually the very pleasantness of Vancouver life that allowed one murderer to continue killing women for so long. The local police certainly seemed complacent about a growing number of disappearances from the Downtown Eastside – almost as if they couldn't imagine that a town like Vancouver might harbour a serial killer. But between the early 1980s and the turn of the century, over 60 women vanished without trace from the area. Eventually, in April 2001 a public outcry led to the formation of the "British Columbia Missing Women Investigation Team" and, following a tip-off in February 2002, they searched the pig farm owned by Robert "Willie" Pickton.

The police immediately found identifiable items belonging to missing women scattered around the farm. This led them to search more thoroughly and they found human bones and bloodstains all over the property. It soon became clear that the bodies had been butchered using farm tools designed to carve up dead pigs. Some bones and teeth had been buried, but other bones, the flesh and internal organs had evidently been fed to the pigs.

Pickton lived with his brother on the farm, but the investigation soon homed in on Robert as the sole suspect. As well as raising and slaughtering pigs, he had set up a registered charity and used the property – the "Piggy Palace" – to host "charity events". In actual fact, he used the government subsidy to hold drunken

RIGHT An aerial view of Pickton's "Piggy Palace": a combination pig farm, slaughterhouse, party venue and murderer's lair. Vancouver police eventually excavated almost every square foot of the property in their search for human remains.

DOCUMENTS

ITEMS 9 AND 10

Thomas Loudamy is a Californian who writes to famous prisoners, hoping to collect their replies. In August 2006 he wrote to Robert Pickton, who was then still awaiting trial for serial killing in Canada. Using the false identity of "Myra Barnett", Loudamy elicited two replies from Pickton; both contained startling insights into the mind of a brutal murderer. Pickton's written replies to Mya Barnett offered a clear hint of what a Jungian psychoanalyst would call a "Jehovah complex": Pickton's rants about other people's "evil ways" and "the terrible anger of God", reflect surviving witnesses' statements that he would work himself into a self-righteous (Jehovah-like) rage before attempting a murder.

ITEM 11

A fax of the search warrant for Seung-Hui Cho's residence. It warrant mentions three bomb threat letters – one found at the scene of the Virginia Tech massacre and two others dating from before the incident. If these latter two threats could have been traced back to Cho in time, it is likely that the VA Tech shooting would never have taken place.

parties, often attended by prostitutes from the Downtown Eastside.

It took five years to build the case against Pickton, including major excavations on the farm; the cost was over $70 million. He was charged with 26 murders and tried on six of them; the remaining 20 were held in reserve for later trials by the prosecutors.

The forensic evidence proved conclusive. For example, an associate of Pickton came forward to tell investigators that Robert had once told him the best way to kill a heroine-user was to inject them with windscreen-washer liquid; the police had discovered an injection needle filled with a blue fluid at the farm. Police also found an unregistered .22 revolver with a dildo fitted over the end of the barrel; one shot had been fired from the weapon. Then, of course, there were the numerous body fragments and DNA matches to missing women found on the property.

But the most damning evidence against Pickton came from his own mouth. In an unguarded moment he told police officers that he had been caught because he had been "sloppy" in cleaning up after his murders. He also told an undercover officer pretending to be his cellmate that he had

MISSED OPPORTUNITY

In 1997, Pickton picked up a prostitute in the Downtown Eastside and took her back to his farm. After having sex, he slapped a pair of handcuffs on her left wrist, and then attempted to stab her in the abdomen with a knife. But she fought back, wounding Pickton in the neck. They both went to the local hospital, where the woman almost died and Pickton was arrested. Yet Vancouver prosecutors failed to press charges against him, deciding that a drug-addicted prostitute was an "unreliable witness". Pickton's clothes and rubber boots were left in an evidence locker and forgotten. It was only years later that they were found to be stained with not just Pickton's and the prostitute's blood, but with that of two missing women.

killed 49 women and that he regretted not making it a round 50.

On 9 December 2007, Pickton was found guilty on six counts of second-degree (unpremeditated) murder and was sentenced to the maximum punishment of 25 years to life in prison. It is believed that

Pickton fed flesh from his victims to himself and to his unsuspecting family and friends. Some may have been sent to a rendering plant – labelled as pork – to be turned into cosmetics. And, of course, his pigs, fed on human meat, were later sold for human consumption.

TOP Willie Pickton, pictured before his arrest. It is believed that Pickton would usually accuse a potential victim of theft when left alone with her. He apparently needed some sort of "justification" to work himself into a killing rage.

ABOVE A picture board showing 48 of the 60 or more women who went missing from Vancouver between 1979 and 2001. Most came from the deprived Downtown Eastside district, prompting accusations that the police had turned a blind eye to the disappearances.

SEUNG-HUI CHO

Virginia Polytechnic Institute and State University (known as "VA Tech", for short) is as large as a medium-sized town, housing over 30,000 students and 1,300 lecturers. With such a big population it's hardly surprising that serious crimes occasionally disturb the otherwise tranquil academic atmosphere. So VA Tech has its own dedicated police force – and it was this that was called out at 7:15 am on Monday 16 April 2007, when shots were heard from the West Ambler Johnson Hall of Residence.

They found two victims: Ryan Christopher Clark, aged 22, and Emily J Hilscher, aged 18. Clark was already dead and Hilscher was dying, both from gunshot wounds. It appeared that Hilscher had been attacked first – in her room – and Clark, who lived next door, was shot as he ran to help her. There was no sign of the murderer.

Believing that the double killing was most likely a crime of passion or perhaps a burglary that had gone wrong, the VA Tech police saw no reason to clear the campus or call a curfew until the killer was apprehended – a perfectly reasonable line to take, but one that they would soon bitterly regret.

The murderer, 23-year-old South Korean-born Seung-Hui Cho, returned to his room in nearby Harper Hall and changed out of his bloodstained clothes. He then deleted all his e-mails from the campus web server, and removed his computer's hard drive. It is thought that he threw the hard drive and his mobile phone into a nearby duck lake, but police dredging has failed to find them. Next, Cho mailed a parcel to the NBC television headquarters in New York. It contained pictures of him waving handguns, a 1,800 word diatribe about how others' lack of understanding had driven him to what he was about to do, and a video clip restating his complaints.

TOP Emily J. Hilscher, aged 18, was Cho's first victim. There was no connection between Cho and Hilscher and, in fact, it seems that Cho did not know any of his victims personally.

ABOVE Shortly after the massacre, flags were flown at half-mast over a floral memorial at Virginia Polytechnic. The 30 deaths count as the deadliest peacetime killing spree, by a single gunman, in US history.

ABOVE South Koreans hold a candlelight vigil to commemorate Cho's victims – the candles spelling out the letters "VT" for Virginia Tech. In fact Cho was culturally more an American than a Korean, having lived in the US since he was eight.

BELOW Seung-Hui Cho wields a handgun in the video footage he sent to the NBC TV. His motivation for the massacre remains cloudy: he himself only mentioned his resentment of "rich kids" and their "debauchery".

At 9:05 am Cho proceeded to chain and padlock all the doors of the Norris Hall Engineering Science and Mechanics Building. Then, wielding two handguns – a .22 Walther P22 and a 9mm Glock 19 – he stalked through the building, shooting at anyone he could see. He killed 30 people and wounded a further 30. It took him just nine minutes. The sound of the police blowing open a chained set of doors alerted Cho to their arrival and ended his murder spree. He put one of the handguns to his own temple and blew out his brains before the police got anywhere near him. None of the victims had any direct connection with Cho.

It later turned out that Cho had obtained his guns and ammunition perfectly legally, despite the fact that he had a history of borderline mental instability. A shy man with a dislike of any physical contact, he had been reprimanded for sending disturbing text messages to female students, and had even been asked by his poetry professor not to write such "sinister" verses. The material sent to NBC does not suggest that Cho had any one reason to go on a rampage, but rather suggests that he was filled with a deep, unfocused resentment.

The "VA Tech Massacre" re-awoke the smouldering gun-control debate in the United States. Supporters of stronger gun-control laws pointed out just how easily a disturbed individual could obtain lethal weapons. The anti-gun-control lobby countered by claiming that, on the contrary, the problem had been that the VA Tech campus had a "no-guns policy"; they said that Cho might have been shot down by one of his potential victims, if only they had been allowed to carry guns to class.

SPREE KILLERS VERSUS SERIAL KILLERS

Understandably, there is some confusion in the mind of the public between "spree killers", like Seung-Hui Cho, and "serial killers", like Fred West or Jack the Ripper. Both are murderers who kill strangers, but serial killers hunt and murder victims over a long period of time, while spree killers murder as many people as possible, as quickly as possible, then kill themselves. Perhaps the easiest way to understand the psychological difference between spree and serial killers is to see a serial killer as an extreme form of rapist – for whom sexual domination of a victim is not enough to feed their ego – while a spree killing is an extremely antisocial form of suicide.

THOMAS HAMILTON

Most school shootings – like the Virginia Polytechnic and the Columbine High School massacres (see pages 44–45 and 48–49) – are a case of disaffected teenagers turning guns on resented teachers and fellow students. The Dunblane massacre was something else altogether: a middle-aged man prowling through a primary school, killing small children.

Thomas Hamilton was born in Glasgow and had a strange start in life. His father had abandoned him and his mother, Agnes, when Thomas was just 8 months old. Agnes then returned to live with her adoptive parents (she herself was illegitimate and had been put up for adoption at birth). To avoid the scandal that was still attached to divorce, they pretended that Agnes had never married. Of course that meant that Thomas could not be seen to be Agnes's child, so her parents adopted him too and his mother pretended to be his step-sister.

It is not known just when the truth was revealed to Thomas, but it may have had a damaging effect on him. He lived with his step-father/grandfather until 1992, but neighbours reported that the relationship between the pair was unhappy: Thomas often bullied and humiliated the old man to the point of urinating in his drinks.

Hamilton's main bugbear was not his family, however, but the Boy Scout movement. He became a leader of the 4th/6th Stirling and 24th Stirlingshire troops of the Scout Association after moving to the Dunblane area in the late 1960s, but had his Scout Warrant withdrawn in 1974. The reason given by the Scouts' County Commissioner was that he was "suspicious of [Hamilton's] moral intentions towards boys". It turned out that when taking scouts on overnight outings, Hamilton had deliberately failed to book accommodation so the boys had to sleep with him in the back of his van. No actual claims of paedophilia had been made, but this situation could not be allowed to continue. Hamilton never forgave this rejection, and the resulting bitterness overshadowed the rest of his life.

Nevertheless, he continued to run his own independent boys' sports clubs: a total

of 15 of them, on and off, between the late 1970s and 1996. Yet the accusations of unsavoury behaviour towards boys continued to dog him. For this Hamilton blamed a cruel conspiracy, orchestrated by the Boy Scout Association – it seems that he not only suffered from borderline paranoia, but he also lacked any degree of self-awareness.

Hamilton looked and behaved like an archetypal child-molester: podgy, balding and bespectacled, he usually wore a "nerdish" parka coat and spoke in an oily and insinuating manner. He also took photographs of the boys in his clubs in their swimming trunks and hung them on the walls of his home. It is true that nobody ever proved any molestation charges against him, but Hamilton never modified

TOP There is no evidence that Thomas Hamilton ever molested any of the numerous boys who had passed through his sports clubs, but his odd demeanour and generally creepy behaviour made many people suspicious of his motives.

ABOVE Hamilton at one of his boys' club gym meetings. There are several security and criminal record checks that must be passed in today's Britain in order to work with children in any capacity. Ironically, Thomas Hamilton, who had no criminal record, would almost certainly have passed any such tests if they had been in place in the 1990s.

his behaviour to reduce the continuing suspicions. One of his final acts was to send out a rambling complaint letter, outlining the "conspiracy" against him – copies of which were sent to the local council, the Secretary of State for Scotland, and Her Majesty the Queen.

Just after 9.00 am on 13 March 1996, Hamilton walked into Dunblane Primary School armed with four handguns – two 9mm automatics and two .357 magnum revolvers. He was also carrying 743 bullets.

Entering the gym, he found the Primary One class of five- to six-year-olds and their teacher, Gwen Mayor. Hamilton killed 15 children, sometimes firing into them at point-blank range. Gwen Mayor died trying to protect the class.

Hamilton then walked out into the playground and fired into a nearby classroom, but luckily the teacher in charge had heard the earlier shots and made the children lie on the floor – none were hurt. Then Hamilton fired at a class hurrying down a corridor. After that he walked back into the gym, pointed a magnum into his mouth and killed himself.

11 children and three adults were rushed to hospital, but one of the children died shortly after arriving. Hamilton had killed 16 children, Gwen Mayor and himself: ostensibly because he was annoyed that people thought he was untrustworthy with kids.

ABOVE Floral tributes left after the school massacre. At least three types of flower have been named for the Dunblane victims. New breeds of rose have been named "Gwen Mayor" and "Innocence"; and a type of wild snowdrop has been named "Sophie North".

BELOW A 9mm Browning HP automatic pistol, of the sort used by Thomas Hamilton at Dunblane. Although such weapons can be used for target practice, they are primarily designed to kill human beings (they are next to useless for hunting animals).

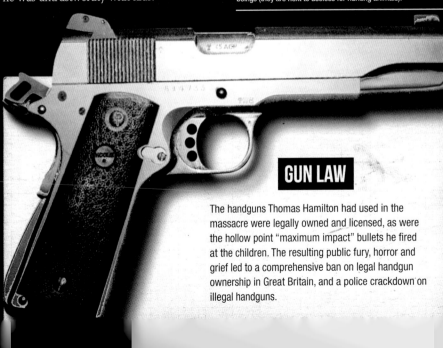

GUN LAW

The handguns Thomas Hamilton had used in the massacre were legally owned and licensed, as were the hollow point "maximum impact" bullets he fired at the children. The resulting public fury, horror and grief led to a comprehensive ban on legal handgun ownership in Great Britain, and a police crackdown on illegal handguns.

HARRIS AND KLEBOLD: THE COLUMBINE KILLERS

The Columbine High School massacre (perhaps the most infamous school shooting in the USA to date) is generally thought to have been the result of two teenagers – Eric Harris, aged 18, and Dylan Klebold, 17 – just running amok with guns one morning. In fact, the assault on the school had been months in the making, with meticulous preparation and planning. If the boys' scheme had run flawlessly, many more students and teachers – not to mention emergency rescuers – would have been killed.

At 11:14 am on 20 April 1999, a small fire bomb exploded in a field 0.8 kilometres (½ mile) from the Columbine High School in the town of Littleton in Colorado. It is thought that this was intended as a diversion for the emergency services. Three minutes later, two 9-kilogram (20-pound) propane bombs were set to explode in the school cafeteria, just as the early lunch sitting was reaching its peak. These bombs could have devastated the area and might possibly have caused a structural collapse, killing yet more people in the library on the floor above. Fortunately they were both duds.

Klebold and Harris were waiting outside the building, armed with shotguns and 9mm semi-automatic weapons. They had intended to spray bullets into the escaping crowd after the bombs went off, but when it became clear that these weren't going to detonate, they stalked towards the school building.

Their first victims were 17-year-olds Rachel Scott and Richard Castaldo, who were sitting on the grass by the entrance doors. Multiple shotgun wounds killed the girl and critically wounded the boy. Then Harris and Klebold entered the building, shooting as they went along. Fortunately, by the time they reached the once crowded cafeteria, the room had been evacuated by teacher Dave Sanders. The killers shot Sanders in the back shortly after leaving the cafeteria, and he bled to death before he could be rescued.

The pair then went up to the library, where they exchanged gunfire with arriving police officers outside the building, shot at cowering students under the tables, and taunted their

ABOVE Eric Harris and Dylan Klebold prowl the deserted school cafeteria, about ten minutes before they decided to turn their guns on themselves. If their plan had run smoothly, and the two propane bombs had worked, the cafeteria would have been a scene of appalling carnage.

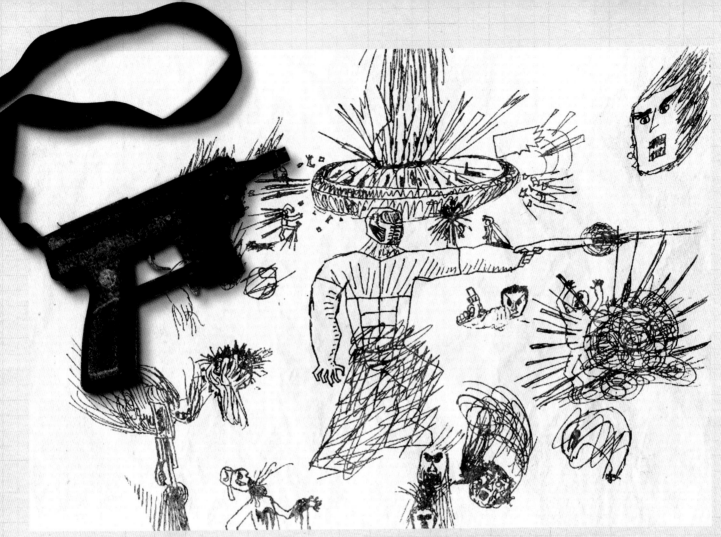

victims. But at 11:38 am, several witnesses heard the killers discussing the fact that shooting had lost its thrill for them. Klebold was heard to say: "Maybe we should start knifing people – that might be more fun."

They left the library and returned to the cafeteria. Clearly intent on self-destruction by this time, the pair shot at the dud propane bombs but they still failed to explode. Next, they went back up to the now evacuated library, passing cowering students on the way but not firing at them. Klebold and Harris shot themselves in the head at around 12:08 pm. They had killed 12 students, aged between 15 and 17, as well as the teacher Dave Sanders. Another 21 students had been injured, many seriously.

In the aftermath of the massacre, many fingers were pointed to attribute blame. Neither of the boys had troubled family backgrounds, so some people accused the school itself. It was said, correctly, that Klebold and Harris had especially targeted "jocks" (students who specialized in gym and sports). Had they been bullied by the jocks? The answer seems to be negative: Harris and Klebold were bullies, not the other way around. Neither were they sad loners who didn't have anything to lose; both had a circle of friends and loving

ABOVE LEFT A 9mm TEC-9 semi-automatic handgun, of the sort used by Dylan Klebold throughout the massacre. "Semi-automatic" simply means that one bullet is fired each time the trigger is pulled; then the gun automatically re-cocks itself. An "automatic" weapon, like a machine gun, will empty an entire bullet clip on a single, continuous trigger pull.

ABOVE A page from the personal journal of Eric Harris. Harris seems to have been the main instigator of the massacre, although Klebold was by no means an unwilling participant. Harris was taking prescribed anti-depressant drugs, which some believe may have enhanced his violent tendencies.

BELOW Harris and Klebold play with guns in a personal video. It has been claimed that the boys' love of violent video games pushed them over the edge. Yet it was only after they were restricted from playing the games, by their parents, that the pair started to plan real violence.

families to whom they had apologized in a final home video.

Evidence as to the boys' state of mind (if not their motive for mass murder) comes from Eric Harris's journal. In this he meticulously plotted the massacre, right down to drawing plans of the school building and considering whether to plant bombs in parked cars – set to go off after the massacre – in order to kill emergency rescuers as they arrived on the scene. The boys had then meant to escape to Mexico.

THE SPEED OF THE MISINFORMATION

It has been widely reported that Harris and Klebold were part of a Goth gang in High School who called themselves the "Trench Coat Mafia". This seemed to be confirmed shortly after the shooting when Harris's father rang the emergency services to say that he feared his son was one of the killers, and that Eric had been a member of the Trench Coat Mafia. However, when the police dispatcher asked him to repeat the gang name, he said didn't know if it was true or not and that he had just heard it reported on the TV. In fact, neither boy was part of the group.

MUHAMMAD AND MALVO: THE BELTWAY SNIPERS

On 2 October 2002, James D Martin, a program analyst at the National Oceanic and Atmospheric Administration, was crossing a car park in the Weaton district of Washington DC. There was a crack of gunshot and Martin was hurled to the ground; he had been shot dead by a single, high-velocity rifle bullet.

Over the following 24 hours – between 3 and 4 October – five more DC residents were killed by long-range sniper shots. James Buchanan was killed at a car dealership in the White Flint area. Premkumar Walekar, a 54-year-old taxi driver, was killed at a petrol station in the Aspen Hill area. Sarah Ramos, a 34-year-old mother, was killed on a bench outside a post office in the Silver Spring district. Lori Ann Lewis-Rivera, 25, was killed at a petrol station in Kensington district.

The last fatality that day was a retired 72-year-old carpenter, Pascal Charlot, who was killed while standing at a bus stop in the inner city. However, he was not the last victim: a 43-year-old woman was also shot while crossing a parking lot in Fredericksburg – a town 64 kilometres (40 miles) south of Washington DC – although fortunately she survived.

On 7 October the killing began again. A 13-year-old boy was shot dead as he got off his school bus in the Maryland suburbs

LEFT James "Sonny" Buchanan, 39, a landscape gardener shot dead as he mowed the grass outside a car showroom in Maryland. The sniper's choice of victims seems to have been entirely random.

BELOW Police impound the sniper's Chevrolet Caprice. Muhammad, holding his rifle, would lie in a hollowed-out space between the back seats and the boot of the vehicle, aiming through a hole in the back of the car.

LIVE WJZ

BREAKING NEWS

CNN ▸ SUSPECTS' VEHICLE HAS BEEN TOWED TO MONTGOMERY CO.

S&P 2.07

ABOVE John Lee Malvo in court. The getaway driver, Malvo once claimed that he and Muhammad had aimed to kidnap children and to ultimately "set up a camp to train children how to terrorize cities." However, neither man ever made any effort to kidnap anyone, as far as the authorities are aware.

LEFT John Allen Muhammad in court. The sniper's motives for the attacks remain uncertain: many believe he was an Islamic terrorist. Others have suggested that he wanted to kill his ex-wife, and murdered the other victims as a way to cover his tracks – however, he failed to shoot his ex. The most likely explanation was that he was a serial killer who was addicted to murder.

of Washington DC. The following day the killer returned to the scene of the boy's murder and left a tarot card with the words "Dear Mr Policeman. I am God" written on it.

On 9 October the sniper killed civil engineer Dean Harold Meyers, aged 53, at a petrol station in the Virginia town of Manassas. Two days later Kenneth H Bridges, 53, was shot dead at a petrol station near the town of Fredericksburg. On 14 October, the sniper killed Linda Franklin, 47, as she loaded her car outside the Seven Corners Shopping Center on one of northern Virginia's busiest intersections.

On 19 October, the sniper attacked what was to be his last victim: a 37-year-old man was shot in the stomach as he left a restaurant in the town of Ashland, 113 kilometres (70 miles) south of Washington, but he survived.

A suspicion that the sniper might be an Islamic terrorist seemed partly scotched by the bizarre tarot card note left at one of the crime scenes: surely no radical Moslem would claim to be God – not even in jest. More evidence to this effect came in

the form of a letter found at the Ashland location. The writer again referred to himself as God, and accused the police of incompetence, adding that it was their fault that people were dying.

The letter demanded a $10 million dollar ransom to stop the killings and added chillingly: "Your children are not safe anywhere or at anytime."

Then, on 24 October, the police caught the killer… or rather, killers: John Allen Muhammad, aged 41, and John Lee Malvo, aged 17.

A member of the public had noticed a car parked for a long time in a road stop on the Virginia Interstate Route 70, and had become suspicious. The police were informed and investigated as a matter of routine. Muhammad and Malvo were found fast asleep in the car, but fortunately the officers did not simply move them on. Closer inspection of the vehicle showed that it had been modified to allow a man to lie inside and aim a rifle while remaining unseen.

Muhammad, who committed all ten killings, turned out to be an ex-US Army

WHY A DUCK?

In an attempt to pacify the sniper, investigators complied with a bizarre demand he had made in his letter to them. A police spokesman read the statement "We've caught the sniper like a duck in a noose" on national television, even though the sniper was still at large. This was a cryptic reference to a folk tale in which an overconfident rabbit tried to catch a duck, but ended up noosed itself.

soldier who had converted to Islam. Lee Malvo, who had only assisted Muhammad, was a Jamaican who lived with the other man and evidently regarded him as a father figure (nobody has ever suggested there was any kind of sexual relationship between the pair). Both were convicted of murder, extortion and terrorism charges in 2003. Muhammad was sentenced to death and Malvo to life imprisonment with no chance of parole. John Muhammad was executed on 10 November 2009.

WOLFGANG PRIKLOPIL

It was the morning of 2 March 1998, when ten-year-old Natascha Kampusch was kidnapped while walking to school in the Donaustadt district of Vienna. Another child, who saw her being dragged into a white mini-van, raised the alarm and a massive police hunt began. Every owner of a white mini-van in the Vienna area was interviewed and this dragnet approach later proved to have been partly successful, in as much as the police did interrogate the actual kidnapper. But investigators failed to follow up on the inconsistent alibi that he gave them, and only discovered years later how close they had been to solving the case.

T he result of this police blunder was that Natascha remained imprisoned by Wolfgang Priklopil, an Austrian communications engineer in his late 30s who fantasized about "owning" a sex-slave. Priklopil locked her in a secret dungeon hidden beneath a cupboard in his garage. In fact, this cell was actually a disused bomb shelter – built by Priklopil's grandfather during the height of the Cold War – so it was relatively comfortable as dungeons go; but it was, of course, cramped, windowless and terrifying for the small girl locked inside day and night.

Natascha was forced to stay in the bomb shelter, without so much as a breath of fresh air, for six months. After that, Priklopil felt confident enough to let her out for periods during the day, when he forced her to do household chores while he watched over her. But he always locked her up again at night and when he went out to work. Over the years he eventually allowed her a small degree of freedom, once even taking her skiing for a couple of hours at a nearby resort; he evidently believed that she was, by this time, totally under his control.

But Natascha wasn't completely cowed. On 23 August 2006, Priklopil ordered her to clean his BMW while he stood guard.

TOP Ten-year-old Natascha Kampusch, in a photo taken shortly before her kidnapping. Priklopil abducted her on the first day that her parents had allowed her to walk to school on her own.

ABOVE The cramped cell in which Wolfgang Priklopil imprisoned Natascha. She has said that he only rarely sexually assaulted her, and mainly seemed to want to "own" someone over whom he had total control.

When his mobile phone rang he moved a few steps away to avoid the sound of the vacuum cleaner. While his back was turned, the then 18-year-old Natascha suddenly found the willpower to run for her life. She was soon out of his sight and begged the first person she met for help. The police were called and shortly afterwards she was under their protection.

Priklopil could have tried hunting for Natascha when he saw that she had escaped. But it is likely the realization that it would be impossible to recapture her without drawing attention burst the psychological bubble in which he had been living his sadistic, domineering fantasy for almost eight-and-a-half years. Overcome by the thought that it was now he who was being hunted and in danger of forced imprisonment, Priklopil went to the Wein Nord station and threw himself under a commuter train. He died messily but instantly. Natascha attended his funeral.

Since her escape, Natascha Kampusch has made a remarkable and praiseworthy return to everyday life. She has resumed her education, has become a prominent animal rights campaigner and has written a book about her 3,096 days as Priklopil's prisoner. In June 2010, it was announced that the celebrated German movie producer, Bernd Eichinger, would be making a film depicting Natascha's ordeal. Several days later, Police Chief Franz Kroell, head of the much criticized investigation into the Kampusch kidnapping, smoked a cigarette on the balcony of his Vienna flat before stepping inside and committing suicide with his police-issue handgun. It is not known if his reported depression was linked to the announcement of the movie, or to the several official investigations into his department's failures in the case.

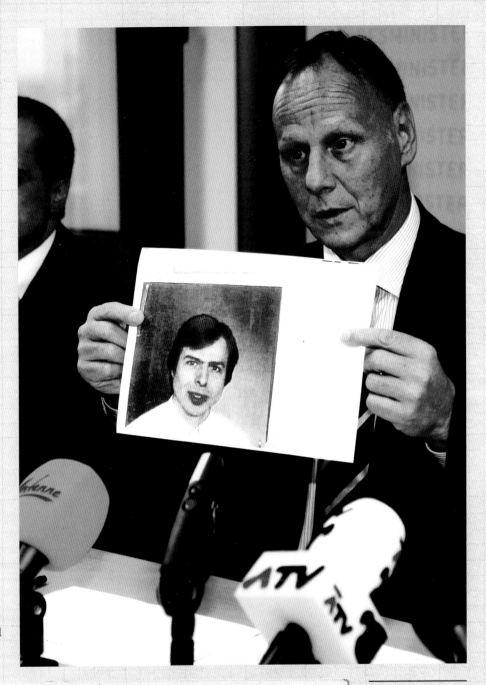

LOVING YOUR ABUSER

Criminal psychologists sometimes call the utter psychological and emotional surrender of a kidnap victim "Stockholm Syndrome" – so called after a drawn-out terrorist siege in that city, in which the hostages eventually started showing loyalty and even affection towards their threatening abductors. This illogical but uncontrollable emotional reaction (noted by the FBI in 27 per cent of abduction victims) is common enough to be exploitable by brainwashers (such as the terrorists who "reprogrammed" the kidnapped heiress Patty Hearst) and by abusive husbands everywhere. It seems to be a throwback to a very primitive human instinct, where a bullying pack leader can command the total obedience, loyalty and even love of its underlings.

ABOVE An investigator holds up a photo of Wolfgang Priklopil for the press. The kidnapper had, by this time, killed himself. Police bungling over the case was to have far-reaching and unexpected consequences.

LEFT Natascha Kampusch after her escape. Her courageous readjustment to everyday life has not been universally applauded in Austria. She has even received hate mail accusing her of shamelessness, and suggesting that she should be locked up again.

JOSEF FRITZL

There are certain people – usually, but not always, men – who have a driving need to dominate others. Since this urge springs mainly from their own deep-felt insecurity, they bully people whom they believe are no threat to themselves – such as their spouse or children. In extreme cases such petty tyrants are so obsessed that any sign of rebellion from those they dominate can drive them to the most insane reactions. Such a man was Josef Fritzl, whose method of controlling his daughter horrified the entire world.

F ritzl was born in the Austrian town of Amstetten. He married Rosemarie in 1956 and they went on to have two sons and five daughters. In 1967, he served a sentence of 18 months for raping a 24-year-old woman in Lintz. Then, in 1977, Fritzl was suspected of sexually abusing his third-born daughter, 11-year-old Elizabeth, yet no police action was taken. Four years later Elizabeth tried to run away from home, but the police caught her and took her back to her father.

Elizabeth waited until 1984 to try to leave home again – since she was now 18 she could no longer be treated as a runaway by the police. But Josef Fritzl was a man with foresight, and had prepared for this inevitable flouting of his parental authority. He hired a builder to extend his cellar with a small complex of rooms, which he himself (being an electrician) wired and concealed after the builder had been paid off. Then, on 24 August 1984, he drugged his daughter, chained her and, after raping her, left her in her newly built prison. It was the last time Elizabeth Fritzl would see daylight for 24 years.

During that time Fritzl visited the secret sub-cellar prison on average once every three days, bringing food and other basic necessities. He also repeatedly raped his daughter and as a result she gave birth to

TOP The Fritzl residence in the Austrian town of Amstetten. For 24 years, nobody guessed that this quiet suburban facade concealed a secret prison – not even Rosemarie Fritzl, who lived in the house all that time.

ABOVE The bathroom of Fritzl's secret prison. He made the subterranean complex reasonably homelike, not least because he would spend time down there with his "second family".

DOCUMENTS

ITEM 12

Almost two years before the Columbine High School Massacre, Eric Harris wrote this level-headed and thorough essay on guns in US schools; scoring 69 marks out of 75. He clearly understood the implications of lax gun security, and later took full advantage of those implications.

ITEM 13

In January 1998, Eric Harris and Dylan Klebold stole a car and were caught by the police. They were sent on a "juvenile diversion" programme, in part to assess them for any deep-seated anti-social tendencies. Both passed the programme with flying colours. In April 1999, the boys conducted the Columbine High School Massacre.

ITEM 14

One of the darkly childish ransom notes which were left at two crimes scenes by the Washington Sniper. Some serial killers love to anonymously taunt the police and some, like the Sniper, like to insist that it is the investigators' fault that victims have died.

ITEM 15

O J Simpson's intake photograph from High Desert State Prison following his conviction for kidnapping. Simpson, once one of the most famous Americans alive, tried to renew his celebrity in 2006 with a TV show called Juiced! – in which he played comedy pranks on members of the public. The show flopped.

seven children. One child died shortly after being born. Of the remaining six, three were secretly deposited on the doorstep of the Fritzl house. A faked phone call from Elizabeth – probably a tape recording – convinced Rosemarie that Elizabeth was now a member of a religious cult and could not be bothered to raise her own babies. So Rosemarie, the grandmother of the "foundlings", dutifully – if gullibly – raised these children for her absent daughter, naming them Lisa, Monika and Alexander.

The other three – Kerstin, Stephan and Felix – were left with their mother/sister, never seeing the outside world except via the television that their father/grandfather/jailor provided for them. It was only on 19 April 2008, when the eldest of these children – 19-year-old Kerstin – fell seriously ill that the whole hideous ménage was revealed. Josef eventually took Kerstin to the local hospital, telling more lies and presenting a fake letter from his "cultist" daughter. Medical staff were suspicious and alerted the police. Fritzl then allowed Elizabeth and his two remaining children out of their cellar, having first made them promise that they would back his story.

UNREFORMED NAZIS?

Asked about both her case and that of the Fritzl children, Natascha Kampusch (see pages 52–53) said that she thinks Austria never fully de-Nazified after the Second World War. She believes that the old National Socialist ideals of absolute authoritarianism and the suppression of female rights are still deeply rooted in the nation's psyche. According to Kampusch, men like Josef Fritzl and her own abductor, Wolfgang Priklopil, are the indirect result of Austria's refusal to fully reject all aspects of Nazi ideology.

However, while visiting Kerstin in hospital, Elizabeth told officials the truth and 73-year-old Josef Fritzl was arrested.

On 10 March 2009, Fritzl plead guilty to coercion, enslavement, incest, rape and the murder by negligence of a newborn baby. He was sentenced to life imprisonment in a psychiatric ward. The authorities accepted Rosemarie's claim that she had

never suspected what was going on, literally beneath her feet. Kerstin recovered from her serious illness and she and the rest of Josef Fritzl's children are said to be doing as well as can be expected in the circumstances. In 2009 it was reported that Elizabeth Fritzl had entered into a relationship with one of the bodyguards who had been provided to keep the gutter press from harassing her.

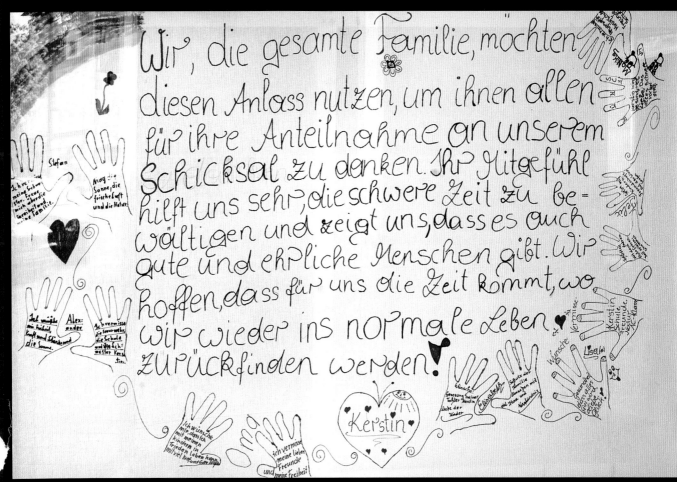

Wir, die gesamte Familie, möchten diesen Anlass nutzen, um ihnen allen für ihre Anteilnahme an unserem Schicksal zu danken. Ihr Mitgefühl hilft uns sehr, die schwere Zeit zu bewältigen und zeigt uns, dass es auch gute und ehrliche Menschen gibt. Wir hoffen, dass für uns die Zeit kommt, wo wir wieder ins normale Leben zurückfinden werden!

TOP Josef Fritzl under arrest. He later said that he had always known "what I was doing was not right, that I must have been crazy to do such a thing, yet it became a normal occurrence to lead a second life in the basement of my house."

ABOVE The poster put up by Fritzl's children/grandchildren in Amstetten. In it they thank those who have helped them since their release and say that "we hope that a time will come for us when we can lead a normal life again."

O J SIMPSON

Just after midnight, on 13 June 1994, 35-year-old Nichole Brown Simpson – the estranged wife of American footballer and movie star, Orenthal James "O J" Simpson – was found dead in the garden of her Santa Monica home. Nearby lay the body of a 25-year-old waiter called Ronald Goldman. Both had been hacked to death with a long-bladed weapon.

Forensic examination placed the double killing at around 10 pm that evening. O J Simpson, the chief suspect, was in Santa Monica at the time of the murder, but caught a flight to Chicago at 11:45 pm. A limousine, booked to take him to the airport, had arrived at 10:25 pm, but found that apparently nobody was at home. At 10:56 pm the driver saw an unidentifiable man enter Simpson's home, shortly after which Simpson emerged, claiming to have been fast asleep in the house for the past few hours.

Later that night, when the police phoned Simpson in his Chicago hotel to tell him that his wife had been murdered, they noted that he did not ask how, when or where the crime had taken place – the usual questions asked by a relative of a murder victim. He didn't even ask if the police had caught the killer. Simpson later claimed to have been so grief stricken on hearing the news that he had crushed a hotel water glass, badly

cutting his hand. However, the prosecution at his trial claimed that this injury had actually been sustained while committing the murders.

Investigators allowed Simpson to remain free until after Nicole's funeral, trusting him to hand himself in for arrest the following day. This proved to be an error of judgement as Simpson failed to turn up. He was soon spotted, however, being driven by a friend in a white Ford Bronco. After a police chase, Simpson was arrested and the car was found to contain a gun, $8,750, Simpson's passport and a false beard.

Starting on 24 July 1995, a 133-day "trial of the century" ensued, with record media coverage. The prosecution sought to show that Simpson was a jealous and abusive husband who would have preferred to murder his estranged wife rather than see her with another man. Their chief evidence for this theory was the cut on Simpson's hand, plus a pair of socks and leather gloves found in O J Simpson's home. The latter

were stained with blood and DNA testing showed it almost certainly belonged to Nicole Simpson.

The defence could only seek to sow a seed of doubt in the minds of the jury in the face of this damning evidence. The police officer who had found the bloodied gloves, Mark Fuhrman, was asked if he ever used the "n-word" (nigger). He replied that he never did. Tapes were then played to the court, featuring Fuhrman using the term with racist abandon. Also on the tapes, Fuhrman admitted to planting evidence to secure convictions.

Another key defence victory came when the prosecution asked Simpson to try on the gloves. They appeared too small for him. Evidence emerged later that the leather of the gloves would have shrunk when the blood dried, but the damage had already been done to the prosecution case. Johnnie Cochran, the chief defence lawyer, told the jury: "If it doesn't fit, you must acquit", which is exactly what they did.

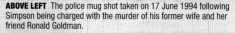

ABOVE LEFT The police mug shot taken on 17 June 1994 following Simpson being charged with the murder of his former wife and her friend Ronald Goldman.

ABOVE RIGHT The body of Nichole Simpson Brown. The blow that killed her almost severed her neck, and had come from within a range of 60 centimetres (2 feet). This suggested she had been killed by someone she knew: few women willingly stand so close to total strangers.

At a subsequent civil trial brought by the families of the victims, Simpson was found guilty of causing the "unlawful deaths" of Nicole Brown Simpson and Ronald Goldman. The deciding piece of evidence turned out to be the murderer's footprints at the crime scene, made by a pair of size 12 Bruno Magli shoes. Simpson had denied on oath ever owning such footwear, but photographs were discovered – taken before the murders – clearly showing Simpson wearing designer shoes of the exact type that had made the prints. O J Simpson's feet were also size 12. Simpson was told to pay compensatory damages of $8.5 million to the bereaved families and $25 million in punitive damages (civil courts in the US cannot hand out jail sentences).

ABOVE O J Simpson tries on the "murder gloves" at his first trial, showing that they were apparently too small for him. It was arguably this moment, more than any other, which planted a seed of doubt in the minds of the jury.

RIGHT O J, in the white Ford Bronco (far right), followed by numerous police vehicles in the now infamous "low-speed" car chase. The LA police were subsequently accused of treating O J with "kid-gloves" because of his fame.

BELOW The example knife shown to the court during the trial process. O J had apparently bought a knife of this sort before the murder, although it could not be found subsequently.

THE LAS VEGAS JOB

On 3 September 2007, Simpson and a group of men entered a room in the Palace Station Hotel-Casino in Las Vegas and stole sports memorabilia from the resident at gunpoint. Simpson was found guilty of multiple felony charges, including criminal conspiracy, assault, robbery using a deadly weapon and kidnapping. In 2008, he was sentenced to 33 years in prison with no possibility of parole until he has served nine years.

RICHARD REID

Britain has produced a number of home-grown suicide bombers during the years of the so-called War on Terror. The "7/7 Bombers", who attacked London tube trains and a bus on 7 July 2005, managed to get past the security services. Others, however, have been caught before they could act, partly owing to lack of training but often because they were almost comically inept. The would-be bomber who has generated the greatest dark humour in the media is Richard Reid, dubbed the "Shoe Bomber". Yet Reid seems to have been the most thoroughly trained and focused British suicide bomber to date, and it was only by a stroke of good luck that he didn't kill hundreds of people.

Born in the South London borough of Bromley in 1973, Reid was the son of an English mother and a Jamaican father. He was mainly brought up by his mother because his father spent much of Richard's childhood locked up in prison. Yet Reid followed in his father's footsteps, being jailed a number of times for mugging in the mid-1990s. It was in Feltham Young Offenders Institution that he found religion and, in converting to Islam, turned over a new leaf.

After his release he started to regularly attend the Brixton Mosque in South London, using his new Islamic name of Abdel Rahim. He was initially an upstanding member of his new community, getting involved in the running of the mosque and learning Arabic so he could read the Koran in its untranslated form. But Richard/Abdel was a highly impressionable man, and soon began associating with more militant Islamists. He indicated the change in the direction of his faith by refusing to wear Western clothes – preferring an Islamic robe, but usually topping this with a paramilitary khaki jacket.

Then somebody paid for Reid to go globetrotting around the "terror hotspots" of the world. Between 1998 and 2001 he is thought to have visited Pakistan, Egypt, Turkey, Israel and Afghanistan. He also went to Belgium, the Netherlands and finally to France. It seems likely that, as well as learning about fundamentalism, he was schooled in the techniques of suicide bombing during this time.

On 21 December 2001, Reid attempted to board a flight from Paris to Miami, but his dishevelled appearance and the fact that he had not checked in any luggage for a trans-Atlantic flight made the French airport authorities suspicious. He was interrogated

ABOVE The passengers and flight attendants of American Airlines Flight 63 restrain Richard Reid after he was spotted trying to set fire to his boot. If his bomb had gone off, it would have knocked a large hole in the hull of the aircraft, almost certainly causing it to crash within seconds.

ABOVE LEFT Richard Reid in prison orange. Like many extreme Islamic terrorists, Reid insists that he is a soldier fighting a legitimate war against the enemies of his faith, not a mere criminal.

SAVED BY SWEAT

Why did Richard Reid's "shoe bomb" fail to go off? It seems that because he was delayed in boarding a plane in Paris for 24 hours, and was sweating so profusely while wearing the bomb, the fuse had become too damp to light with a match held in his shaking hand.

BELOW United States Attorney, Michael Sullivan, makes an official statement shortly after Richard Reid pleaded guilty to all charges. Despite the subsequent tightening of international airport security, our two main defences against fanatic bombers remain good intelligence networks – to detect and arrest terrorists before they get close to their targets – and simple good luck.

ABOVE RIGHT The remains of the "shoe bomb" after it had been defused by bomb squad officers. On an economic level, Reid's attack was a big success: the few moments that it now takes to remove your shoes for security inspection before a flight, multiplied by millions of passengers every month, adds up to a vast waste of time and money for the Western nations that Reid hates.

and, although he refused to answer certain questions, was allowed book a flight for the following day and then leave the airport. If he had been thoroughly searched during this interview, the investigators might have found that one of his boots was packed with explosives.

On 22 December Reid boarded American Airlines Flight 63 to Miami without incident. Shortly after the in-flight meal had been served, a passenger complained to stewardess, Hermis Moutardier, that Reid was lighting matches. Moutardier warned him that smoking was strictly forbidden and he promised to stop, but a moment later she saw that he was hunched over, apparently trying to set light to a boot that was resting on his lap. Reid pushed Moutardier away when she tried to stop him, and then bit the thumb of another stewardess, Christina Jones. Moutardier threw some water over Reid and nearby passengers managed to restrain the 1.9-metres (6 feet 4-inches) tall would-be suicide bomber. They tied him up with seatbelt extensions and a doctor injected him with tranquilizer from the plane's medical kit.

Then Flight 63 made an emergency landing at Boston, Massachusetts, and Reid was arrested. The startled authorities found that he had more than enough explosive in his boot to have caused the plane to crash, and it was only the fact that the fuse had repeatedly failed to light that had prevented detonation.

Other failed British suicide bombers have pleaded "not guilty" to charges laid against them, arguably undermining their cause in the eyes of the world by denying their wish for martyrdom. Reid, however, remained loyal to his anti-West beliefs, pleading guilty to all charges (including the "attempted use of a weapon of mass destruction" – the airplane itself if it had been caused to plummet from the sky). In October 2004 he was sentenced to life imprisonment with no chance of parole.

TED KACZYNSKI

On 25 May 1978, a small parcel bomb wounded a security guard at Illinois' Northwestern University. This was the first amateurish attack made by the serial killer who later became known as the "Unabomber".

Between May 1978 and December 1985, the Unabomber is known to have sent out nine, fortunately non-fatal, parcel bombs. Two were intercepted and defused, but the others injured 18 people, some seriously. One of these bombs, which wounded United Airlines president Percy A Wood, earned the bomb-maker the media nickname "Un A Bomber,' which was later simplified to the "Unabomber".

December 1985, in Sacramento California, saw the first fatal attack. Hugh C Scrutton tried to remove a package left lying in the car park behind his computer rental shop. It exploded, killing him. This bomb had not been delivered by the Postal Service; it had been simply left in the parking lot. It seemed likely,

therefore, that the killer had put it there in order to watch the result of his handiwork.

The next bombing followed the same pattern. On 20 February 1987, a bomb was left in the parking lot outside a computer firm in Salt Lake City. The owner of the company, Gary Wright, drove into the lot, got out of his car and kicked the package out of the path of his tyres. The resulting explosion blew off his leg.

A secretary had seen this last package being left by a man, and she described him to the police. Perhaps as a result of his description being published, the Unabomber ceased activity for six years. When he struck again he did so using his original method of delivery: the US Postal Service.

On 22 June 1993, a parcel bomb badly injured Dr Charles Epstein, a leading geneticist

at the University of California. Only swift medical aid saved his life. The next day a similar parcel bomb badly hurt computer scientist Dr David Gelernter of Yale University. He too survived, but only after extensive medical treatment.

On 10 December 1994, a parcel bomb killed a New York advertising executive, Thomas Mosser. One of Mosser's corporate clients was the Exxon oil company – responsible, in many people's eyes, for recklessly polluting the environment.

Less than five months later, on 24 April, timber industry lobbyist Gilbert B Murray picked up a parcel. As he lifted the package, one of his staff members joked: "It's heavy – must be a bomb." The blast destroyed Murray's head and upper body. Fortunately, he

ABOVE The issue of *The Washington Post* for 19 September 1995, which carried the Unabomber's 35,000-word environmentalist manifesto. The *Post* and the *New York Times* published the manifesto on the direct request of US Attorney General, Janet Reno.

ABOVE The Unabomber's 3 x 4-metre (10 x 13-foot) cabin, in the process of being moved by the police. It was in this tiny cabin in Montana, that Ted Kaczynski lived... and made his bombs.

BELOW LEFT Theodore Kaczynski's police mug shot. The Unabomber, a former university professor, is one of the most academically accomplished serial killers on record. Most serial killers have above-average IQs, but few have been particularly successful in putting that intelligence to any positive use.

BELOW RIGHT The Unabomber's brother, David Kaczynski, reads a statement to the press while their mother wipes away tears. David's painful decision, to report his suspicions about his brother to the police, undoubtedly saved lives. Serial killers rarely cease killing until they are caught.

MONSTER OR ECO-WARRIOR?

It has been noted that the Unabomber's 1995 "manifesto" contained ecological demands that are today common policy for many mainstream political parties. Was he an environmental warrior then, fighting to save the planet? Yes and no. Few can doubt that Ted Kaczynski was genuinely passionate about the environment, but he was also a sadist who went out of his way to see two of his victims blown apart. Given that context, it seems certain that his "manifesto" did more harm than good to the ecological movement.

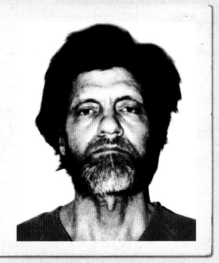

was to be the Unabomber's last victim.

In April 1995, the Unabomber sent copies of a lengthy letter to *The Washington Post* and the *New York Times*, threatening to blow up a passenger jet if it were not promptly published. The "manifesto" proved to be a rambling diatribe that attacked big business, environmentally damaging government policies, scientific research and progress in general. It was plain that the Unabomber believed that all development since the Industrial Revolution

was dangerous and damnable.

David Kaczynski read the Unabomber's manifesto and realized with horror that it sounded exactly like the rantings of his hermit-like older brother Theodore. With natural misgivings, David Kaczynski informed the FBI, who raided Theodore's home and found plenty of proof that he was the Unabomber.

Theodore J Kaczynski had been a brilliant academic – in 1967, at just 25 years old, he had been appointed Assistant Professor of

Mathematics at Berkley University, California. But in 1969, Kaczynski suffered a total emotional breakdown and had subsequently become a recluse in Montana, churning in hatred for the modern world. Living in an isolated log cabin, Kaczynski believed he followed a life that was in tune with nature, making bombs which included parts carefully hand carved from wood.

In 1996 Kaczynski was sentenced to four life sentences, with parole permanently denied.

INDEX